NOT
A SOLITARY
WAY

NOT
A SOLITARY
WAY

Evangelism Stories
from around the World

Edited by
Raymond Fung and Georges Lemopoulos

**MISSION
SERIES**

WCC Publications, Geneva

Cover design: Rob Lucas

Cover photo: WCC/Peter Williams

ISBN 2-8254-1096-9

© 1992 WCC Publications, World Council of Churches,
150 route de Ferney, 1211 Geneva 2, Switzerland

Printed in Switzerland

Contents

Introduction

RAYMOND FUNG

"And I... will draw all people to myself"

John 12:32

Some years ago I accompanied a group of Orthodox friends on a visit to the churches in China. It was their first exposure to Chinese churches.

I remember in particular a worship service in a rural town. The congregation consisted of three former house churches. A year before, an old Baptist church building had been made available for their use. So here they were, about a hundred Christians and their friends, and our little visiting group was worshipping with them.

The preacher was a woman in her eighties. She was almost inaudible. The loudspeaker didn't quite work, switching itself off and on at whim. But we were given the Bible text and we made out something of what she was saying.

There was a choir, half of them blind. As we learned later, the town used to house a large Methodist home for the blind. The home was taken over by the government in the 1950s. However, through all these forty years, the residents here had kept their faith and, in a sense, their faith had kept them. That Sunday afternoon, they were singing praises to the Lord with gusto.

After the service, the visitors sat down with the leaders of the congregation for a conversation. Among the questions we asked was: "What is your greatest need as a congregation?" The response was prompt. Without the slightest hesitation they said: "We need a full-time pastor."

For the moment, the congregation was making do with a city pastor who came once every three or fourth months. The journey was hard for the old man. The time he could afford to give them was grossly inadequate, and the arrangement was expensive. "What we need is an ordained pastor."

I pressed them: "Why do you need an ordained person? You have been worshipping God in house groups for over twenty years under very difficult circumstances. And God has taken good care of you. You have been faithful. You managed well without any ordained leadership. What do you need a pastor for?"

I must admit, at this point, I was only half-playing the devil's advocate. My Baptist background was showing, too.

Our friends from the congregation found themselves wordless. They looked at one another, hoping somebody would respond. But no one did. These people had a clear sense of their need. But apparently they had never thought of articulating a reason for it.

Then Georges Lemopoulos, one of the Orthodox friends, spoke up. With some hesitation he suggested: "Maybe, just maybe, you want an ordained pastor because your congregation wants to be, and to feel itself as being, part of the world church of Jesus Christ?"

That did it. Our friends were happy. Several nodded their heads vigorously. An old woman clapped her hands. All of them were smiling as if they had seen a new light. Georges, who had never been to China before then, had found the word for their heart's desire. His Orthodox sensitivity and Orthodox theology were right on target on this occasion. Very probably he had provided the right answer.

The incident is important to me and, I believe, to the churches. That's why I am happy to help compile this collection of evangelism stories from Protestant, Roman Catholic and Orthodox sources. One learns so much more from stories of people coming to faith in Jesus Christ described in different ways.

Having read and re-read the stories in this collection, for me one simple truth stands out clearly and powerfully: it is Jesus Christ who draws a person to himself. When a person comes to faith, it is primarily because he or she is being pulled to Christ, and not because he or she is being pushed by somebody else. The dynamism is that of a movement towards something better, rather than of a movement away from something that is bad.

That is also the story of the evangelization of the apostles. Jesus issued the invitation "come and follow me", and Peter and his brothers followed him. The biblical records have not given us much more than that. We do not know what exactly happened. What we can legitimately claim to know is that Jesus appeared and invited them to join him. What Jesus had to offer must have surely appeared attractive and worthwhile.

In this collection of stories, we find a similar dynamic, although the process of human response varies. Some respond to Jesus within a relatively short period of time. Others take months, even half a life-time. Some make a decision and stick to it. Others make a number of decisions through many years. In some cases, the stories conclude open-ended. Readers are left unsure of the outcome. But one thing is true of the varied experiences here — all the stories tell of how Christ drew men and women to himself. In one way or another, they had been confronted with something that was infinitely better than anything they had seen or known, something that made eminent sense to the good side of every one of them.

But what of judgment? What about sin and guilt, and our awareness of them which has played such a dominant part in the church's articulation of the process of conversion to Christ?

These too are found in abundance in the stories. The awareness of personal sin and sinfulness is present here very much as a human response to grace. Immediately or much later, it invariably follows one's encounter with Christ. In the presence of Christ, one comes to see human reality differently, including one's own. Thus there is a clear awareness of judgment. But it is not judgment leading to despair. It is judgment in terms of forgiveness and hope, because the judgment has been brought about by the presence of Christ. If Christ were not present, there would not be such awareness of judgment. Or there would only be the sort of awareness that leads to despair. Christ make us become aware of our sins. By this same action, he also makes forgiveness and hope available to us.

The story of Jesus by the Lake of Gennesaret in Luke 5 makes this point clear. Peter, James and John were about their business of fishing. They had worked hard all night long and had not caught anything. Jesus came to them and helped them land a good catch. At this point, Peter fell on his knees before Jesus and said: "Go away from me, Lord! I am a sinful man!" There is no mention of Jesus reminding Peter of his sinfulness. Peter came to the realization that he was a sinful man in Jesus' presence. The story ends with Peter and his partners pulling their boats up on the beach, leaving everything, and following Jesus.

It is significant that in all the four gospels, there is not a single instance of Jesus saying to an ordinary person: "You are a sinner" or words to that effect. Except when Jesus was addressing the religious leaders of his time (what a threatening thought!). However, as in the story of Peter by the lake, people who came close to Jesus often became aware of their sinfulness all by themselves.

The awareness of personal sin is an essential part of a person's faith journey with Christ. It is an awareness prompted by grace, supported by grace and leading to growing in grace. When a person becomes aware of personal sinfulness, he or she is already embraced by grace.

From this collection of stories, repentance does not seem to be a once-for-all event either. Repentance is a process, or more precisely many events within a process. Imagine how many repentances Peter must have gone through.

Let me conclude with a theological plea. I look for a new theological paradigm for our understanding of who a Christian is. Traditionally, when we think on this subject we have recourse to the image of a circle. Whoever is inside the circle is a Christian. Whoever is outside is not a Christian. With some churches, the circle is small. With other churches, the circle may be very large. But small or large, it is a circle we all draw. There are people who are in and they are Christian. There are those who are outside and they are not Christian. I would propose that we go for a different image. Instead of drawing circles, let us draw arrows. There are arrows moving towards the cross, and there are arrows moving away from the cross. There are arrows that are fairly close to the cross but pointing away from it. There are arrows far away from the cross but pointing towards the cross.

This way of thinking may make much better sense of the experiences recorded in this collection of evangelism stories from Protestant, Catholic and Orthodox sources.

The Corridors
of Maasai Society

MARION FAIRMAN

My husband and I have been to Kenya in East Africa seven times, first as volunteers in mission, later as visitors to our son's family when he was a missionary among the Maasai. It is only natural then that we keep thinking of the people in Kenya, especially of the Maasai, the ones we know best of all the tribes.

We can understand the core of Maasai culture by watching them work near the end of the day. About six-thirty, the sheep and the goats are brought in by the children. In the village, the women sort them out, putting the lambs and kids into holding pens. While they wait for the men to bring in the cattle, the women rekindle the little fires smouldering all day on the floor of their straw and dung homes.

Just before dark, the herds come in. The women bring the calves to stand beside the cows, a move to encourage the flow of milk. Milk is important to the Maasai; it is the basis of their diet. The men, still carrying their spears and staves, move around, looking after any animals that are injured or show any sign of disease. When the men and the herds are all inside, the women pull in the branches that serve as the gate in the thorn fence surrounding the village.

After the work is finished, the families go into the houses to sit around the fire. They will drink milk, perhaps eat a little maize meal or boiled potatoes. The men tell the stories of how it has always been with the Maasai. And the children listen, absorbing the history and tradition, until they fall asleep. The men and the women sit a little longer around the fire, discussing the important happenings of the day.

This pastoral existence is far from most other Kenyans' way of life. But God's word is the same word to the Maasai, these semi-nomadic people.

It was with this understanding that our son and his family went southwest of Nairobi into the Rift Valley to live with the Maasai. They were supported by MASI, Maasai Action for Self-Improvement, and worked under the Presbyterian Church of East Africa and as overseas associates of the Presbyterian Church (USA).

From 1970 to 1980, in an area two-hundred miles long and eighty miles wide, eight to thirteen churches had been started. But in the five years between 1980 and 1985, forty-four Maasai congregations were planted. During the early days, if the leaders of a village wanted a school, Samuel Pulai, the one Maasai Presbyterian minister in the area, would send a Christian young man with perhaps a year of village schooling to teach the small children. This method established schools but few churches. Because of the social structure of the community these young men would find no audience among the elders. So effective evangelization of the larger community was stifled.

Some of these young men had the faith and the tenacity to "hang in", to earn a record of integrity in dealing with the people, and to win a hearing through years of service to the community. When, after a long time, they had established a place in the community, they became effective Christian leaders.

Later, a more useful pattern emerged, a plan to strengthen the existing ties of age group and kinship and sub-sections of the Maasai. Through these relationships, then, bridges were built which crossed age and clan barriers. In turn, as the winsome nature of the Christian life became apparent in the village, more people were ready to hear the gospel. This approach is less formal than putting an evangelist in the school, but it follows the corridors of Maasai society. It is far more productive and allows for effective nurturing and disciplining of believers.

As a consequence, out of the groups within the community, strong natural leadership emerges. Samuel Pulai and Tim Fairman, our son, then took the more mature and capable men and women as their key leaders who would receive weekly teaching of the scriptures. Each of these is responsible for several junior evangelists. And all of them are responsible for training the lay people as they follow Christ.

I'd like to tell you about three of these evangelists. One is a woman named Ng'oto Rachel, a special person. She is in her late fifties, perhaps in her early sixties. She's not sure because Maasai can't tell you the year they were born. But they can show you the age group they belong to, those who have undergone the rites of passage together. Ng'oto Rachel, or the mother of Rachel, is a widow with three daughters who live in more remote areas of Maasai land. She is raising her grandchildren because there is a Christian school near her village.

One fall, Samuel Pulai and Tim arranged a retreat for the senior evangelists. They wanted to give them an experience beyond the isolated situation in which they live. They rode in a truck to the Pastoral Institute where the Presbyterian Church of East Africa provides facilities for classes and retreats in the old Zambesi hotel on the road north of Nairobi.

At the first supper, Ng'oto did not show up. Tim excused himself and went to look for her. He knocked on the door of her room on the second floor and asked if he could come in. She said "Yes". Tim went in; the room was dark. He asked where she was. She was sitting on her bed in the corner. Tim felt along the wall, found the switch and turned on the light. Ng'oto was amazed. She didn't know there were such switches. When the night falls in Maasai land, only the house fires hold back the darkness of the night.

But the Maasai are also holding back the onslaught of confusion. They are caught in the pull between modern Kenya and tribal tradition. If a child dies in infancy, the mother will neglect her next child, allowing its hair to grow long and tangled. If she does not attract attention to this baby, she reasons, perhaps it will live.

The Maasai women also know what it is to be in bondage. From her village to another Ng'oto walks, carrying on her back a container of water, five or six gallons, as a gift to the women in the other village. As an older woman, she can speak freely to other Maasai women; she has walked their way before them. To grow up as a girl in Maasai society means to work, carrying the water and wood, preparing food and tea, carrying as she works a younger brother or sister on her hip. At eight or nine, a girl becomes sexually active and by the time she is ten she accompanies the warrior group as a "lover". At puberty, a girl is circumcised and married to a junior elder, a man at least twice her age.

A Maasai woman never has a say about her own life. As a wife, she comes under the constant and sometimes cruel supervision of her husband. When Ng'oto's husband died, her husband's brother, or any other elder in her village, became her "boss". A woman like her, with no son to care for her, lacks all status. In the gospel Ng'oto discovered that through Christ she is a daughter, a child of God. She heard of Jesus caring for and lifting up Mary Magdalene, Mary and Martha, and the woman taken in adultery. She knows that Jesus loves her and gave his life to bring her to God. Talk about liberation! Set free, Ng'oto has given her life to help penetrate the darkness in Maasai life; from village to village she walks, bringing the light of love and understanding to Maasai women.

Another evangelist is Peter. His Maasai name is Seketian ole Sakuda, but many Christian Maasai take biblical names when they are baptized. He and Tim are age-mates, both in their late thirties. Peter and Tim frequently take to the villages the film "Jesus", a dramatization of the gospel of Luke provided by Campus Crusade for Christ. Hundreds of languages around the world have been dubbed in, and it is one of the few films with a Maasai sound track. Maasai adults are largely illiterate and cannot read the scripture. The film is popular.

But to set up for the showing requires great physical effort. In the afternoon, Tim and Peter load the stuff into the truck — the film, the projector, the generator, the gasoline for the generator, the speakers, the screen, the cables and ropes to tie down the screen. As the sky darkens, the people gather, and Peter sits down in their midst. One night when Tim started the film, the wind was blowing so hard the screen blew over six times. Finally, the two biggest men were chosen to sit on top of the ropes to hold the screen up.

About eleven o'clock that night, when they were in the third reel of the film, Tim's back was hurting from sitting on the ground. The dust and the dry cow dung were blowing in his eyes and burning. He started to dream about the coming Christmas season when all of our family would be together. But then he noticed Peter. The same dust, the same manure, were blowing in his eyes; he was just as tired. Yet he was sitting there, animatedly pointing out all the things going on in the movie, telling who this person was and who that person was. And Tim confessed his own pain and discomfort didn't seem all that much any more.

Jehoshaphat ole Nagirro, a warrior before he became a Christian, is an older man responsible for some widely scattered villages. In the community of Olmararoi lives a politically appointed chief who told the people: "Baptism is bad for Maasai." The Maasai themselves have no village chiefs. Each village consists of a family or several families who have come together for their mutual welfare. The leaders of the society are the junior elders (those older than the warriors) and the senior elders, the older and wealthier of whom have the most power and influence. They meet in council and decide the issues facing the village. Groups of villages form a community and are governed by these councils working together.

Outside of a hostile village Jehoshaphat saw six elders wrapped in blankets tied on the shoulder; he sat down with them under a tree to talk. The women of the village had heard him teach in another village. They came out and asked him to pray for them. The elders frowned and shook their heads. But Jehoshaphat was unwilling to say he wouldn't pray as the women had asked. And so he stood, closed his eyes, and prayed. When he looked up, he saw that four of the six old men had slipped out. The two who remained couldn't leave — one was blind and the other was crippled.

Jehoshaphat said goodbye to the women and started walking to his home village about ten miles away. He kept wandering off into the bush, then back onto the path — and then off again. He went down into a valley and up the next hill. There he stopped and looked back. He was filled with such pain because his people were rejecting what God wanted to give them that this warrior-evangelist began to cry. When I heard his story, I remembered the time when Jesus looked across a valley to the city where his people lived and cried for them because they were like sheep without a shepherd.

Yet, seed was planted that hard day. A year later, the crippled man, the most influential elder of his village, asked to be baptized. When Tim baptized him and his family, the cripple took the name Abraham and his senior wife took the name Sarah. Four years later, in 1986, Abraham set aside some land near his village, ground on which a church is to be built for the community of Olmararoi.

One afternoon, Jehoshaphat took my husband and me, along with Ng'oto, Peter and Tim, on a walk to sample evangelism, Maasai style. At the first village, Ng'oto's home, the women, children, and Maasai men too old to be out with the cattle, sat down on the ground under an acacia tree, shaded from the hot African sun.

Jehoshaphat read the scripture; Peter began to preach, building on what the Maasai traditionally believe. They believe that Enkai (God) created the world, that he is omniscient and omnipotent but that he is not intimately involved with his creation. To the Maasai, God is up there and out there. When they hear from the prologue to John that God has come to share life with his people, the message strikes them as extraordinarily good news. One of the names some Maasai Christians use for God is Enkai Nalagua Nataana (the distant God who has come near). Maasai also believe that God once gave the Maasai a child who grew up among them to become Oloiboni, their first prophetic/religious leader. And so in the Christmas story, they hear and accept that God has given his people another child, Emmanuel, to grow among them and to lead them.

In the Old Testament stories, they hear of the Israelites, a tribe remarkably like the Maasai, a patriarchal people who also had flocks of sheep and goats and cattle and who, like themselves, were driven from place to place by their need for grass and water. Maasai women who pray to God for a child become as one with Sarah and with Rachel. Maasai men who have been shepherds all their lives respond to David, the shepherd king, and to the one of David's line called Jesus, the ultimate Olchekut Supat, the Good Shepherd whom they can understand and follow.

In Tim's experience, the Maasai understanding of sin varies. In some situations they acknowledge that all people sin; at other times they seem unaware of sin. But they are all bound by fear of curses and resort to amulets and charms. Most Maasai religious ceremonies involve sacrifice and ritual participation carried out according to exact standards. One man is chosen to represent them all; that man must be ceremonially clean — one who is not a murderer, one who has never had sex with a woman of his mother's age group, one who is not left-handed, one who has a good reputation. In Jesus, they find a high priest, one who can represent them with the sacrifice needed to restore them to a good relationship with God.

As Peter preached, I watched a dung beetle roll his giant ball of eggs past a woman's bare foot; two kid goats wandered among us and curled up under a man's bent legs; scavenger dogs sniffed warily around the edges of the group. Through the grass came four women, bent double under great loads of firewood gleaned from the scrub trees. Like other Maasai women, their heads were shaved; they wore bead decorations draped around their necks, wrapped around their arms, hung from holes in both their upper and lower ear lobes. Next to me a baby slept in a sling against his mother's back. Many children played on the ground, chased the dogs, splashed in a deep puddle of manure and mud.

When Peter had finished, Jehoshaphat prayed again; as Ng'oto led spirited gospel songs, the women swayed to the rhythms of their ancestors. And then we started for another village, walking single file. I was last, following Ng'oto on the path which twisted through the thorn trees. As we clambered up a steep grade over rocks, storm clouds rolled in over the Ngong hills. Ng'oto, bent under the weight of the water she carried, glanced up and smiled, glad that rain was coming to the dry land. She began to sing softly; the others joined in. The words "Yesu Christo" floated back to me, a name understandable in every language.

I wonder if this Maasai experience does not speak to all of us of the nature of evangelism, indeed, of the Christian life. It is not a solitary way; it is walking the narrow path with fellow Christians, enduring with them the thorns, the rocks, the heat — even the mud and manure of life — yet joining with them in the joy of service, sharing with them the tasks of everyday life, singing with them a song of praise for the water of life, freely offered by our Lord Jesus Christ.

Two Stories from Malaysia

ROBERT HUNT

The first story begins many years in the past, indeed before the second world war. But its fruition came only many years later. Some time in the 1930s, a Rev. Ting was appointed to one of the churches in Sitiawan. While he was there, a young woman came seeking a job as a domestic helper. She had come, like many others, from a China torn by war and economic crisis to seek some living for herself and her relatives back home. Like most of these women she was unmarried, and had no intention of marrying. Outside the home her recreation was meeting with her companions at one of the "vegetarian associations" which serve as social club, religious centre, and ultimately retirement home, for the Chinese women who gave up the normal option of married life. Rev. Ting spoke to her about Jesus and treated her well, perhaps better than a woman of her position could normally expect in those desperate days.

In the years after Rev. Ting left Sitiawan, she went on to other jobs in that town and the surrounding area. Her story really only begins again for me in 1985. Late in the year she came to the old parsonage where she had worked and asked to speak to the pastor, whom she had never met. In her poor Mandarin (she was a Foo Chow) she explained to Rev. Lim that she felt that she would soon die. She would prefer to die in a Christian old folks' home rather than in the vegetarian association home. Rev. Lim, who did not speak Foo Chow, called a woman from his church who did, Mrs Teh. The old woman told Mrs Teh that she had decided she wanted to die in the arms of Jesus, about whom Rev. Ting had told her some fifty years ago. That afternoon Mrs Teh shared more with her about this Jesus, and before the afternoon ended the woman professed her faith in him, and surrendered her life into his hands. In the meantime, Rev. Lim had contacted the sisters of a Catholic old folks' home. In a few days the arrangements were made, and she went to live there among her new Christian brothers and sisters. Six months later she died, in the arms of the Jesus she had heard about from Rev. Ting all those years before.

The second story is a bit more involved. I have changed the identity of the man at his request. Although he has told this story publicly, it embarrasses him to think it might be more widely known.

Mr Teow (we will call him) was raised in a strict Confucian home, where the highest values were stressed. As he matured he embraced (additionally) a stricter form of Buddhism which rejected much of Chinese folk religion and Taoism. Nonetheless, even as he became a respected leader in the community, and a prosperous manager with extensive responsibilities, he remained in some ways dissatisfied. In particular he felt he did not have a close enough and loving enough relationship with his teenage sons.

As it happened, several of his employees were Christians. When they took tea together in the mornings they would often discuss religion. He was happy to be present and take part in these discussions, indeed he felt it good to encourage them. He, for his part, shared his beliefs and happily discussed the beliefs of others. As time passed, many of the Christians he employed began to develop deeper spiritual lives and became more involved in the life of their church. Some joined charismatic groups. Gradually the way in which they discussed their religious faith changed. It began to captivate Mr Teow. They talked less about their beliefs and more about the experiences they were having in their groups and in the church. Mr Teow was especially drawn to the kind of family relationships he heard about, and to stories of the miraculous healing of many broken relationships. Before long, to his surprise (and, so they tell me, their surprise), these Christians were witnessing to Mr Teow in a more forthright manner, inviting him to attend various evangelistic meetings and participate in a Bible study in which they were taking part.

At this point events began to occur in such a way that Mr Teow now feels they were providential. His sons began to be involved somewhat with one of the Christian youth groups, although they themselves were not Christians. His employees visited his family one night and together they had an impromptu Bible study. Then, rather suddenly, Mr Teow became very sick and had to be hospitalized. It appeared that he had serious blood pressure problems which were both difficult to diagnose and to treat. During his time in the hospital he began to think through his own life and faith. He also met an unexpected and unusual witness to Jesus Christ. It was a woman who washed the floors, a person who could speak to Mr Teow in broken Malay. But she assured him that she would pray for him. Then, only a few days after she had met him, she stopped him in the corridor of the hospital. "God has healed you, you are wasting your time here," she said. The doctors did not concur until two days later, when they discharged him for the last time. For those two days his new friend, whose name he never learned, reassured him that God had told her he was healed.

When he returned home he plunged into a period of reading the Bible and reflection. In those free days he read furiously, completing much of the Old and all of the New Testament. The testimonies of his friends seemed to match the testimony of the Bible to Jesus. Before long he was ready to return to work, and anxious to hear more about becoming a Christian.

As it happened, there was an evangelistic meeting the weekend after his return to work. He resolved to go and see if this might not answer some of his questions. It seemed odd, and embarrassing in a way. Indeed he worried about going a great deal. As attractive as the testimonies of the Christians were, they were in many ways alien to his own self-understanding. They were warm, and full of feeling, so much so that he felt embarrassed to hear them sometimes. He worried that the meeting might lack any dignity at all. He had been struck powerfully by the testimony of the sweeper in the hospital, but it too seemed odd, especially the confidence she had that God had healed him. It almost seemed stupid, a simpleton's faith. Even as he prepared to leave with his wife for the rally, he fleetingly imagined arriving at a hall full of toothless washerwomen, carrying on in who could know what way. Nonetheless he went, and was relieved to find a congregation full of his acquaintances. But as they sang he began to feel something. He began to sense around him the kind of warmth he had felt in his employees' testimonies. People were joyful, and he felt happy to be with them. The sermon reflected the kind of confidence he had heard from the cleaning lady, but in a different key. He began to feel confident that what he had heard about Jesus, and had read for himself, was true. That night he responded to the invitation of the evangelist and put his faith in Jesus Christ.

A few months later, after attending membership classes, he was baptized in a congregation of a mainline denomination and briefly gave his testimony. Not long after he shared this testimony again with a large group in the company for which he worked. Since then his Bible reading has continued unabated, and his involvement in the church has deepened.

I have met him several times. I doubt he has outwardly changed much. He is a very reserved man, almost shy. His actions were always of the highest calibre and they continue to be looked upon by the community as exemplary. But he tells me that really everything has changed. His family is now much closer, and he really feels the love between himself and his sons. And more, he feels he now has something to offer others, something he never had before. Indeed, it is he who now witnesses at the coffee hour, exhorting his employees to a deeper faith and more active love.

Both stories are typical in certain ways of evangelism here. The process of coming to faith is often long, especially among people who already are more than passingly religious according to the traditions of their own culture. And more often than not it seems to be the warmth of the Christian community and Christians at worship together which attracts people and ultimately convinces them to put their faith in Christ. Precisely because such warmth cannot be communicated in just a night or two, I have found that real conversions here are seldom solely the result of evangelistic rallies.

Perhaps it is worth noting, if only for reflection, that there are really three distinctive aspects of the gospel to which people respond here. While all three are found in churches, I think it is true to say that different groups emphasize different aspects. Among the very poor, especially the Indians who are the poorest of the poor here, there is a strong attraction to the gospel presented in terms of Jesus' power over the powers of the world. "Signs and wonders" are stressed in many of the Indian churches which are growing most rapidly. Many Indian Christians regard this as the core of the gospel. Among the Chinese in rural areas, and those in the cities who still speak Chinese exclusively, it appears that churches focus on the message of God's anger with sinners, the forgiveness available in Christ Jesus, and the need to live a holy and sin-free life. It is a tradition going back to John Sung, who is still remembered as an almost legendary figure among Chinese Christians, but its effectiveness as an evangelical tool remains unabated. Among the urbanized Chinese and Indians, especially those of the middle class who speak English and Mandarin in preference to their dialects, it appears that the most attractive presentation of the gospel comes from charismatic groups such as the Assembly of God. There is a stress on the gifts of the Spirit, including healing. But even more than this, it seems to be worship, which is highly emotional and involves the worshipper in a loving and very optimistic community. These are people who hope "we will reign, reign, reign" in the words of one of the most popular songs.

There are some reasons, both obvious and obscure, why different groups respond to different aspects of the gospel message. On the positive side it is noteworthy that at least some Christian groups know how to communicate effectively the gospel among Malaysians. Negatively, there is a tendency within each group of churches to focus on the aspect which "works" evangelically to the eventual exclusion of the other aspects. And it appears that only the Roman Catholic Church has responded seriously to the aspect of the gospel which calls for suffering as a witness among people who may never respond with loyalty or even thanks.

A Coptic Family in the Church

MAURICE ASSAD

It was Sunday. The bell of the village church was ringing, calling the Christian peasants to worship.

Botros and Maria hastened to the church with their son Mina and their daughter Agapi. They entered the church and Botros proceeded to the altar. As he knelt down he emptied himself completely before God, in reverence and awe. This was the way he had always expressed his repentance and his gratitude, the way he had offered thanksgiving and glorification to God, his Creator and Saviour. Since his early childhood, Botros had gone to church every Sunday with his parents.

Botros had never gone to school, and he could not read or write. Nevertheless, he had gained a basic knowledge of the Christian faith from the liturgical life of the church.

Following him, his wife Maria came with the children to the iconostasis. Both children loved the icons. Each of them lit a candle and placed it before the icon of the Virgin Mary carrying the child Jesus. They opened their purses and put some money in the offering box. Their grandmother had taught them that this was very important: every gift of money for the work of the church, the propagation of the gospel and the assistance to the poor and needy was, in fact, a gift offered to God himself.

Agapi asked her mother to hold her up so that she could reach for the icon and kiss the Virgin and the child Jesus. Through this particular icon Agapi had developed a personal relationship with Jesus and Mary.

"Blessed is the kingdom of the Father and of the Son and of the Holy Spirit, now and for ever, and unto ages of ages." With this solemn doxology, the priest announced the key to the entire celebration: the entrance into the kingdom. To bless the kingdom of God meant for the family to love it as one's most precious possession, because this was for them eternal life in communion with God and in loving obedience to his divine will.

Botros, Maria and the children followed the prayers very attentively. They sang with the rest of the congregation. Mina whispered to his little sister: "Stay quiet. We are now in the house of God. Listen carefully, because this place is full of angels and saints." Maria was happy that the children were enjoying the liturgy.

The children were totally involved in what was going on. They were fascinated by the lights, the icons, the liturgical vestments of the priest and the deacons, the incense, the candles, the altar and all its surroundings. All this had a meaning for them. Everything inside the church was speaking to them. If they were able to put all this in words, they would certainly have affirmed that the modest altar of their small village church represented the whole creation; that the prophets, apostles, saints and martyrs they could see in the icons formed, with all the people of God, present and absent, dead and alive, the communion of saints; that the lights and candles were means to understand the illuminating presence of the Holy Spirit...

The family loved the hymns and chanted them with the congregation, just humming when they did not know all the words. As Botros and Maria sang, they submitted all their being before God. When they were young, they had been instructed in the faith and grown into the tradition of the church, handed down through the liturgy. Tradition and liturgy for them were not theoretical knowledge, but a living experience that they shared with the rest of the community of worshippers throughout the liturgical celebration and in everyday life.

The congregation listened with attention to the readings of the day from the epistles of St Paul and from the Catholic epistles. As the gospel was read, everybody stood with reverence listening to the words of God with open minds and hearts. Throughout the readings Jesus was with the congregation in this small church, revealing himself to each person and the divine will to the world. Therefore, to our family, the proclamation of the gospel in the church was a sacramental act, a form of communion with God, a real mystery in and through which they felt united with God.

Then the priest went to the pulpit and began preaching. This also was proclamation of the divine word, the announcement of the good news. They listened carefully to the sermon. The priest spoke clearly and in simple words. They understood what he taught them. Even the children were able to comprehend what the priest was saying. Although they were simple illiterate people, they had learnt many parts of the Bible by heart through the readings and the preaching during the liturgical services.

"Peace be with you!" "And with your spirit!" Joy and peace filled the hearts of Botros, Maria and the children, and of all the congregation.

"Let us lift up our hearts," called the priest. The congregation responded from the depth of their hearts: "We lift them up unto the Lord." Botros and Maria became totally involved in the liturgical act with all their being: mind, body and spirit. They offered themselves completely to the Lord, who had offered himself to them.

During the whole liturgy, the Holy Spirit had been the instructor of the entire congregation. The Spirit filled their hearts with spiritual illumination. *"Kyrie eleison* — Lord have mercy," they chanted with all the people assembled in the church.

The celebration of the liturgy continued. The family, together with all the congregation, had now become entirely immersed in a new dimension that had allowed them to see the ultimate reality of life: Christ is present... The whole family lived moment by moment with Christ: at his birth, throughout his life, his crucifixion, death and resurrection.

The priest started the eucharistic prayer: "... In the night in which he gave himself for the life of the world, he took bread in his holy, pure and sinless hands, and when he gave thanks, and blessed it, and sanctified it..." While the celebration of the eucharist continued, Botros and his family stood before God, listening to and experiencing this offering of the body and the blood of Christ for the life of the world.

As the family received the holy communion with the rest of the congregation, their whole being was transformed in an inexplicable way. They were in communion with God and with all the members of the church. They belonged to one another as members of the one body of Christ. Indeed, they were now so much like the early community which St Luke has described in the book of Acts. They had been renewed through Christ whom they had received into their whole being.

Botros, Maria, Mina and Agapi came out of the church. Nevertheless, they did not leave the church behind them. In fact, they took it with them in their hearts. They knew that now they were sent into the world to bear witness to the kingdom of which they were partakers in the liturgy. The Christ, present during the celebration, had now to be present in their home, in their village, in their labour, through their attitude and witness.

They had the assurance now that the Holy Spirit, who always changes the ordinary bread into the body of Christ and the group of worshippers into a real community, would also change their own words into words of truth; their lives into an unceasing witness to the risen Lord; their simplest daily efforts into a commitment to the kingdom.

They must now conduct themselves as free persons in Christ, "constantly renewed in the image of (their) creator" (Col. 3:10).

Something Began
to Move Our Lives...

SLAWOMIR MAKAL

Our venture started in the seventies. It is a story of witnessing to the gospel through encouraging the full participation of youth and lay persons in the church and in missionary activities, and enabling them to play their prophetic and apostolic role. But let me start at the very beginning of our long journey.

A sower went out to sow... In the Warsaw metropolitan church of St Mary Magdalene, after the Sunday liturgy, a group of young people — mostly students — are invited by a young man to a meeting in the basement of the church. The young man starts the meeting with a word of prayer: "O, Heavenly King, Comforter, the Spirit of truth..." He continues with the reading of the Sunday gospel.

Immediately after the reading, the young man goes on to interpret the passage. I am deeply moved by the way he explains the message. It is simple enough to be understood by everyone, and it has a strong impact on my mind and soul. It is clear he knows what he is talking about, and he speaks with a strong spiritual and emotional involvement. The speaker's personality and, even more, the sense of community — all of us gathered together as Orthodox Christians — impress young people of different ages, jobs and interests. The leader invites us to ask questions. Those who have something to say are mostly those who have already acquired some knowledge and experience from previous gatherings.

After the discussion, the young people have some time for informal conversation, friendly exchanges and getting to know one another better. The singing of a joyful hymn to the Virgin Mary, *Axion estin...*, marks the end of the meeting.

As he sowed, some seeds fell on good soil... I regularly attended these meetings in the last years of my studies. I was really impressed by the leader, the atmosphere, and the quality of the discussion, the sense of community, its openness and frankness.

These meetings have gone on for about ten years. The young man who has been the soul of these gatherings was a graduate from the Christian Theological Academy of Warsaw. He started this work among the Orthodox youth of our country after completing his post-graduate studies at theological schools in Moscow and Zurich. He has had no support from the church authorities; in fact sometimes their reactions were discouraging.

The members of our youth group, however, were enthusiastic, and continued their efforts to understand the true nature and vocation of the laity. They began to organize various kinds of activities, like excursions and camps. In our small local Orthodox church, facing various problems and difficulties which threatened its very existence, something was now happening, after a very long period of stagnation and passivity.

Thanks to the young man's efforts, the first Orthodox youth fellowship emerged in 1979. The Orthodox students of the Christian Theological Academy in Warsaw and the students of the Orthodox Seminary in Warsaw received the blessing of our metropolitan to form the Circle of Orthodox Theologians (COT). This was a historic moment, for now the youth activities had both the necessary organizational framework and the needed recognition from our church hierarchy. And one should keep in mind that this was the period preceding the well-known August 1980 political events in Poland.

... and seeds brought forth grain! The young members of the COT decided to organize a youth pilgrimage to the Monastery of St Martha and St Mary on Grabarka Hill in eastern Poland.

Grabarka is famous among the Orthodox in Poland as a holy place with a long and rich tradition. It is known as a place of prayer and repentance, reputed for miraculous recoveries from many diseases. After the second world war, a small convent was established there. Thousands of people from the entire country meet at the convent on the day of the Feast of Transfiguration.

One day in May 1980, early in the morning, three young men arrived at the monastery after a night-long train journey. They had come to visit the mother superior of the monastery and to get her permission to organize the pilgrimage. They were sorry when they found out that the mother superior was not well. But, despite her illness, she warmly welcomed the visitors and agreed to offer hospitality to the young pilgrims.

Would it ever be possible for us to describe what we felt when we went on our first pilgrimage and spent a weekend together in that holy place? We were forty young Orthodox praying, singing, discussing and experiencing together the joy of Easter, addressing one another with the traditional Easter greetings: "Christ is risen!" "Indeed, he is risen!"

This was the first youth event that began the tradition of Orthodox youth pilgrimages to Grabarka during the Easter period. In a few years the number of pilgrims rose to around two thousand. In an astonishing way, this holy place began to transform the life and witness of Orthodox youth.

Nowadays, this initiative enjoys the co-operation and assistance of the holy synod of our church. Our bishops join the pilgrimage, and their presence and concern for the youth are a source of encouragement. Several bishops and priests from sister churches also take part part in these pilgrimages.

During the pilgrimage in 1981, the youth gathered in Grabarka applied for permission to create a church lay youth organization. Soon after, the Orthodox Youth Circle (OYC) came into being, and assumed overall responsibility for Orthodox youth work in Poland. Some months later the Orthodox youth bulletin was born. The OYC became a member of Syndesmos, the world fellowship of Orthodox Youth Organizations.

Sower and reaper can now rejoice together! The Orthodox youth movement in Poland is now ten years old. The young leader whose work led to its formation has been elected a bishop. Some of the participants at those first gatherings are now priests and monks, some are engineers and teachers; and one has become a deputy in the parliament.

Without those ten years of committed work, we could not have established the official Orthodox Brotherhood in Poland, which is today the recognized body of Orthodox laity in our church.

Being Present in the Muslim World

ROBERT McCAHILL and DOUGLAS VENNE

1. The experience of Robert McCahill

On 20 January 1986 I passed my ninth year in Tangail. When I came here early in 1977, my purpose was to be of assistance to the poor in whatever way I could, and to insert myself into this Muslim and Hindu community as a Christian brother. These have been nine wonderful years. I have been consoled to have been able to help many poor persons in ways that they themselves want. Trusting and affectionate relationships between Muslims/Hindus and myself have been built and maintained. The signs of love for the poor and full respect for others' faiths have been made, and are appreciated by the people. I judge that it is now time to move on to another place in Bangladesh in order to make the same signs to new persons.

I intend to leave Tangail shortly in order to settle in Kishorganj town. Archbishop Michael has encouraged me. I ask you to pray that my new beginning will be blessed by the Lord.

I feel that the Lord is urging me to leave Tangail and settle in a new place. That inspiration is the reason for my plan to transfer. But, on the practical level, why should this missioner start again elsewhere? Are the opportunities for doing good works and giving Christian witness in Tangail less now than they were in the past? Quite the contrary. In fact, the more involved I become with more people, the greater are the opportunities to assist and to save. There will always be sick/poor persons who need a brother's help.

However, I believe the sign of Christian love has been made here for a sufficient duration of time. That sign has been seen by two groups: namely, the poor and the non-poor. On the one hand, many poor persons have experienced disinterested love from a source they never expected — that is, from a foreigner, an "Englishman", whose image in this culture is normally of someone who is greedy for liquor and sex. The poor, in turn, have reciprocated with kind words and deeds towards me. They call me "mama" (maternal uncle), "dadu" (grandfather), "bhai" (brother). They often invite me to eat with them. (Are there any more elaborate ways for persons to express gratitude and affection than those?) Poor persons whom I've never met approach me filled with trust that, even though we are strangers to one another, I will surely help them in a way they need to be helped. They have heard, through others, of the rare desire of the brother (or the saheb, the doctor, the cyclist) to freely assist and accompany them to medical treatment. I am privileged to be a source of hope for the poor.

On the other hand are the non-poor; that is, the middle and upper classes, who also observe what I am doing. They approve of my work with and for the poor. In the beginning they were largely suspicious of my intentions. I am told that in conversations among themselves they acknowledge that the brother is "doing" religion. Some apply to me the Islamic belief that "the key to heaven is love for the poor". Once I was informed that a "maulavi" (religious teacher), while lecturing a group of "imams", cited "the brother's work of searching out and carrying patients to hospitals" as a model for their own service to the poor. By most indications, the people of Tangail understand it is love that motivates this missioner, and not the desire to convert Muslims. In summary, although one slightly fanatic person violently opposes me, the people in general regard me as a friend, and not as a threat, to Muslims.

The place I have chosen to start again, making signs of love and hope and respect, is the town of Kishorganj. By bus, Kishorganj is twice as far from Dhaka as is Tangail (i.e. four and a half hours as compared to two and a quarter hours). Its population of 100,000, approximately 90,000 Muslims and 10,000 Hindus, is at least as large as that of Tangail town.

I do not know what the Lord is holding in store for me in Kishorganj. Nor did I know what the future would hold when I boarded a bus bound for Tangail nine years ago. As I rode the bus towards Tangail I asked the Lord to insert me into that unknown place before day's end. I had not the faintest idea about where I would spend that first night. The Lord inspired a fellow passenger (Nurul Islam, a complete stranger) to invite me to meet a friend, who introduced me to another friend, who took me into his house for the next six weeks. I was surprised, grateful, and conscious that God was working everything out for me.

One logistical problem that transfer to Kishorganj entails has to do with burial. A few years ago, after Pakku Miah and I had already cemented our friendship (through my concern for his health, which led me to bring him to a doctor; and his concern for my health, which led him to invite me for meals), we struck a bargain. That is, if Pakku were the first to die, I would bury him; and if I were the first to die, he would bury me in the bamboo grove behind his brother's widow's hut. Maybe that agreement will have to be suspended when I go to Kishorganj.

I intend to keep in contact with friends in Tangail, however, through mail and periodic visits. As 90 percent of my Tangail friends are unable to read and write, perhaps I should look for literate persons who will receive mail for my friends, and read it to them. Many of the Tangail poor are so much a part of my life that I will be happier for continued contact with them.

Among those friends are many women. In 1975, before we came to Bangladesh, we were told that we would not be able to work with women; their menfolk would not allow it. After serving the poor for several years, I realized that already I was dealing with women as much as, or more than, I was dealing with men. Besides the fact that I am able to work effectively and lovingly with persons whom society tends to ignore (i.e. sick/poor women), the trust their menfolk place in me is a joy to experience. The great trust that husbands, fathers and brothers of women place in me is yet another signal that the sign I came to make has been adequately made in Tangail. Henceforth, the same process will begin in Kishorganj; that is, working first with sick/poor men, for as long as it takes to build trust, after which they will permit me to help also "their" women. As women in Bangladesh are less free and more neglected than men, I believe that to help women in any substantial way is to work for justice and peace.

Several years ago Archbishop Michael asked the Maryknollers in Tangail to evaluate their apostolate among Muslims and Hindus in Tangail. One of his questions was: "Why do you live together?" I answered that it would have been difficult to begin working among Muslims, and even more difficult to sustain that early work, without the presence and support of like-minded fellows. It seems to me that now it is time to experiment with living outside a community of priests. The inspiration I feel now is to start anew in an untried place, and to hope that someone from that place will want to join me. I think I have learned during the past eight enjoyable years in the Tangail Maryknoll Fraternity that the people of Tangail are neither impressed nor edified by our community life in their midst. On the contrary, some people seem to suspect that life in a male community denotes oddness. Frequently I have been asked by friendly, curious persons: Whom do you live with? When I reply that I live with my religious brothers, there is silence. The questioners drop the topic that they imagine can only embarrass me. It appears to me that the suspicion of homosexuality easily comes into some people's minds when they see unmarried mature men living together. In order to present an understandable living arrangement to my new neighbours in Kishorganj, it might be fitting for me to consider living with a Bengali or two, to whom the local people could put their private questions about the missioner's life.

Another reason for wishing to start again in a new place has to do with my age (48 years) and the psychology of the modern age. Nowadays men and women are advised to change jobs before ten years pass, in order to rekindle enthusiasm. Fresh starts are occasions for grace.

In the new place I rented a room for six dollars per month, furnished it with a single-burner kerosene stove, a candle holder, a clay water jar, a washpan, plate and glass, a sleeping mat and a wardrobe as elaborate as my surroundings. Doug kindly supplied a slightly leaky pressure cooker; he knows I have not the patience to deal with any other sort of cooking. Then I set out to get to know the Kishorganjis...

"Who are you? What do you do?" the people want to know. I explain: "I am Brother Bob, a Catholic Christian missioner. I am here to serve the sick/poor. Service to the needy and love for all persons is my religion. Christians believe that Allah makes happy those who serve the needy." Implied in my reply is a message for any who wish to understand it: this Christian missioner is your brother. I wish you well. I appreciate your faith and your culture. There is nothing about you that I seek to change except that which you also wish changed. I will gladly try to help you free yourselves from whatever debilitates you, that is, free you for living useful and happy lives.

There are no other foreigners in Kishorganj. Not now. But, between 1916 and 1930 the Nazarene Christian Mission of Kansas City, Missouri, maintained a girls' high school in this unlikely place. Only Allah knows what were and are the effects of that mission effort. One thing is clear, however. There is fellow-feeling in Kishorganj. Did the Nazarene Mission contribute to that attitude? Or is it solely due to the strivings of Muslims and Hindus to live harmoniously close together? Or is it for reasons I have yet to discover? The place fascinates me.

So do the people. I wish you could meet many of them. Like Chaytali. She is fourteen, the last of 14 children, and one of the three who have survived. Both parents are gone. Chaytali stands five feet tall, weighs 64 pounds, has fine features, a light complexion and a winning smile. Six months ago someone humiliated her so severely that she wanted to die, for which purpose she drank some nitric acid from a jeweller's shop. The attempt failed, but as a result of it she can no longer swallow food and lives on milk whenever she can get some. "I want to eat rice again!" she declares. First, though, she'll have to have some work done on her oesophagus. I volunteered to be her brother; she prefers to call me "Dadu" (Grandpa). She assures me that she never went to school and is "dumb". However, she is anything but that. I marvel at the intelligence and resourcefulness of this sweet scrawny Bengali lass. Now she wants to live and not to die. She can use a little help from her friends.

2. The experience of Douglas Venne

You know the story of my stay with Mazam Ali's family after his son Rahiim died. When I brought him to the hospital he was too weak to walk. He rode on my back. As we sat on the steps of the outpatient clinic he would say to just anyone passing: "This is my friend, Brother Doug." It was so genuine. He was admitted to the hospital where he stayed for six weeks. For some reason or other he had a stroke which paralyzed his left side. Yet to the other patients he would say when I came to visit: "Here's my friend, Brother Doug." My heart welled up. When I took him from the hospital, he was so frail and had no balance. Yet he was happy to be going home. Getting off the bus at the village, I carried him piggyback across the school yard. You would have thought he was a king returning home from victory. All the kids greeted him, he bowed left and right. I could feel importance surge through him. At home he still couldn't eat well. His mother tried to massage some life back into his limbs. On his second day home I went to Dhaka to see a physiotherapist, a friend of mine, to get help. When I returned, the neighbouring kids shouted: "Rahiim is dead." I felt I had lost a member of my family.

After Rahiim's death, I spoke to Mazam Ali: "I will take Rahiim's place in the rice field." Mazam Ali and his family were very poor and certainly needed someone to supply the labour that Rahiim had been doing, but he said: "I can't pay you anything." "That's OK," I answered, "I will work for you for nothing." For the next year and a half, I squatted down in the rice paddies, working full-time each day all week just as if I were a member of Mazam Ali's family.

I received one meal each day and sometimes two. They were ready to feed me. I ate whatever food they themselves ate. The people knew I took Sunday off as my prayer day. Each evening, I went home to live with my Maryknoll companions in their rented tin house, three miles away. A year and a half passed. On the occasion of an Islamic revival meeting, Mazam

Ali was castigated. The organizers of this meeting put pressure on the village leaders to have Mazam Ali tell me to leave.

The leaders, to this day, never asked me to leave the village. What they did was threaten Mazam Ali and his family with very difficult sanctions if I continued to work with him. So poor Mazam, with sadness in his face, asked me to leave. His family and others never announced any intention to become Christians, at least I never heard about it. What I did learn later from a couple of men who attended the meeting at which Mazam was threatened was that because I had Mazam Ali with his wife and a few other couples to our house during the Christmas season for a snack and a trip to the movies, then I would have invited them to be Christians as well. The leaders, however, as far as I know, never asked Mazam whether I proposed he become a Christian, nor did they ask Mazam whether he wanted to be one. They told him that such was my purpose. To this day, no leader has asked me to stay out of the village. On the contrary, after a year and a half, my relations with the leaders are quite cordial and I even help Mazam Ali at times in his fields.

The Conversion
of Sonny Teresa

JOHN WATSON

Sonny Teresa works today as the accountant of a well-established Christian community in England. "Sonny" is a nickname, the kind of contraction which Westerners often use when they meet a strange tongue; it has some relation to her given name in Farsi, the language of Persia. "Teresa" is the Christian name she chose when the writer baptized her in the name of the One God, Father, Son and Holy Spirit.

Sonny Teresa was born a Shi'ite Muslim in Iran and born again, according to a serious Christian understanding of these words, in Britain. In the reflections which follow, the names Sonny or Teresa will be used where they seem to fit. The central motif of Sonny's story is "acceptance". It has been used by more than one Christian as a synonym for Christian existence itself and as an umbrella word which encompasses the proclaiming of the gospel and its reception. Sonny was once accepted by some Christians and she took the rather dramatic and heroic step of accepting God in Christ.

The notion of a pluralist society is a relatively new one in Britain. Sonny made her spiritual decision in an environment where it was possible to make free political and religious choices. The present writer's experience of conversion from Christianity to Islam and from Islam to Christianity goes back to the 1950s. Sonny's baptism took place in a very different climate which was paradoxically more dangerous and more free at the same time. The 1980s was not a time of freedom though it boasted that it was.

Every Muslim who has come to know God in Christ has, in our experience, pointed to a sincere personal Christian love as the key to that decision. A Christian who has acquired the spirit of peace and who shows it is far more effective than any argument. In the West we meet many brilliant Iranian refugees. It seems that they are initially motivated by emotions and later by a cognitive process. This does not apply only to converts to Christianity. The writer has taught a number of Iranians who have been "converted" to Marxism, in a life-changing manner, which had nothing to do with "understanding" Marxism. At the time of Teresa's baptism another young Iranian woman, of high intellectual ability by any standards, was "converted" to communism. To quote her personal testimony: "I believe in Marxism-Leninism but I have much to understand." She could not have known that she was echoing a great Christian theologian.

As far as Teresa was concerned, the beginning of her pilgrimage was a friendship based upon love and prayer of such a depth that it would overcome every difficulty. Spiritual understanding does not come overnight and it does not even come through reading the Bible. Teresa was accepted as a person in her own right. She was never "conversion fodder" and we did not rush it. We prayed that she would be made ready to accept Christ's invitation. This meant listening. It meant a conscious refusal to attempt an explanation of the whole gospel in one day. The growth was to be slow and steady or not at all. Christian concepts were never introduced until she asked first.

There are many temptations which present themselves to a Western Christian working in a multifaith community. It was in such a community that Sonny and I met. The greatest temptation is to assume too much, and the first difficulty in the community was ignorance of Shi'ite Islam and the world of an Iranian. To understand Teresa and her conversion it is essential to understand both from her point of view. Sonny came from a reasonably well-off family in Iran. She had been raised with two important ideas which are common currency in Iran.

First, the Iranians are not Arabs. The old nineteenth-century labels which sharply distinguish between the "Semitic" Arab Muslim and the "Aryan" Persian Muslim had a compelling urgency in Sonny's childhood world. She has said that Iranians of her age were raised to be as proud of their pre-Islamic history as they were of Shi'ism. The Iranian calendar dated back to the reign of Cyrus the Great, king of kings, described in Isaiah's prophecy as "God's anointed". The history and culture of ancient Persia were emphasized in the Iran of the Shah. Sonny recalls that the racial purity of Aryan Persia was emphasized alongside a contempt for the Jews who were unclean. Hitler was admired. She remembers the massive celebrations which Shah Mohammed Reza Pahlavi forced upon Iran in 1971 to commemorate the 2500th anniversary of Iranian monarchy, a tradition which he could not really claim to represent. Persepolis, the site of the celebrations and a centre of the Achaemenid empire, was quite near to Sonny's home. She was proud of the 1971 spectacle and recalls its darker side which not only denied the place of the Jews but also marginalized other Iranians like the Armenian Christians and Bahai "heretics" who were to suffer so terribly in the future.

The second invariable fact of Iranian experience is that of Shi'ite Islam. A summary, however bald, must be attempted. Sunni Muslims are the orthodox followers of the Sunna — the way — of Muhammad the Prophet who died in 632, leaving no succession. Islam prospered under three Caliphs but the fourth Caliph, Ali, the cousin and son-in-law of Muhammad, was opposed. Ali was martyred in 661 and Hassan, his son, in 669. Ali's younger son, Hussein, was martyred soon after, and through these three a permanent division of Islam was born. This was the Shia, or the party, of Ali. Shi'ism has survived into our time with its teaching of martyrdom and vicarious suffering. Iran is the largest Shi'ite country. Some Shi'ites live in Iraq, Syria, Pakistan and, of immense importance now, in the Lebanon. In Iran a strong belief in imams, the successors of Muhammad, has survived. Khomeini was a member of Muhammad's hereditary class of Sayyids. Some Muslims in Shi'ite lands believe that the Ayatollah Khomeini was the twelfth Imam, the Awaited One, who disappeared in the ninth century and had now returned, more than a thousand years later, to deliver Shi'ites from misery. The Ayatollah (from "aya" — *sign* of God) is appointed by a college of Islamic clergy.

Before I met Sonny I had lived through the Iranian revolution with student friends and had come to understand very precisely that the Islamic world, led by the Persians, was a leader in science and the arts when Europe was in the dark ages. Persian music and literature includes some of the world's classics and its poetry is legendary. The Persian contribution to astronomy and mathematics led to European technology. Sonny has often told me that everyone was expected to know and love the poets. She is a gifted artist like her grandfather but, as she says, "it is normal to be good at art; it is in your blood". Many Iranians are excessively proud of Persian history whilst claiming to be internationalists and Marxists. It is not much to say that the only Aryan racialists I have known were Iranian Marxists. Sonny did not belong to this group but she enjoyed the rewards of her family's wealth which enabled her to travel to Europe and have a good time. Like almost every Iranian I have known she was a heavy smoker and drank alcohol moderately in defiance of Islamic culture. She was a modern woman!

The religious and political enthusiasms of Iranians cannot be exaggerated. Iran is a land of great beauty and its many different people are alive with individual tribal cultures and political passions. The British frown on the discussion of religion and politics in a social setting. This does not make sense to Iranians. Politics is probably their favourite topic of conversation. I have spent more hours than I care to recall discussing Iranian politics with students and schoolchildren sent to the West. Religion is a natural topic of conversation. The Persians have been a religious people since the dawn of time. Long before Jesus and Muhammad, the halls of Persia echoed to the sound of religious debate. One of the world's great primal religions of earth, air, fire and water existed in the plains below the Zagros mountains of Iran. Religious conversation with Iranians is as natural as it is with Egyptians. They have a background which demands our respect.

Sonny's first religious instincts were awakened when she was fourteen in Iran. In a milieu where dreams have always held a place, she found herself standing in the middle of "nowhere". There was a beautiful clear pool. It brimmed with crystal water. The pool contained a wondrous goldfish. She stood by the pool in the stillness. In her own words: "I heard a voice saying, 'Why don't you believe in me?' I answered, 'Because I have not seen any sign.' The voice asked, 'What do you want?' I replied, 'Do the impossible — make the fish fly.' The fish instantly turned into a bird and flew away into the sky. Then I believed. I told others to believe. The end of the dream was peaceful. I saw myself dying but there was no pain and fear. I knew that I had met God in my childhood dream. Years later, when I became a Christian, I remembered that dream. If that dream was a promise then God was true to his promise, for he met me and brought me home and did the impossible by healing me and giving me new life."

London is far from the clear air of the Iranian countryside. It was in London that God brought together a group of people to work a new miracle, the kind of miracle of evangelism which God is working every day. Sonny came to England from Shiraz in Iran. She studied in London and graduated in business studies. Like many students, her life was self-indulgent. Her interests were cultural; she loved plays and good films.

Sonny now reflects that she had absorbed an intensely material understanding of religion. In the Shi'ite calendar, the month Muharram is significant. Sonny had often seen the faithful parade on the ninth of Muharram, dressed in black and beating their chests whilst crying "Hussein! Hussein!" On the tenth, which is the anniversary of Hussein's martyrdom, men stripped to the waist, beating themselves with chains or leather straps embedded with pieces of glass. The intense passion plays of "Taaziehs" are performed. Forty days later the death of Hassan is recalled. Ali, his wife Fatima and the imams are also mourned with emotional displays. The focus is vicarious suffering and the virtue of compassion. Apart from the palpable reality of suffering, Sonny recalls the material ecstasy of the Shi'ite "heaven" as it was taught to her. Heaven was very real and materialist in rewards. It was a garden of beauty — the lost paradise of more than one of the world's living religions. Suffering and paradise were both materially real. Religion was a very materialistic business.

In London Sonny met a number of Christians. She lived for some years in a Christian hostel as a paying guest. The people running the hostel were living a kind of Christian communal life. Sonny observed their quiet daily prayers. She heard continual references to the Bible and so she read it to prove that it was wrong! Like many before her, she finished her reading with a very different and slightly bewildering impression.

When Sonny and I sat down to talk about religion, it seemed sensible, in the light of our knowledge of Shi'ite Islam, to concentrate on the substitutionary character of the death of Jesus on the cross. I shall always be grateful to Sonny for putting me right. It was love that was drawing her to Christ; the love and prayers of one particular young woman and of others in our community. Sonny expounded the death of Christ to me in terms that a theologian would call the exemplarist theory of the atonement except that it was not a theory to her: "O dearly, dearly has he loved and we must love him too." It was the love of God that overwhelmed Teresa.

It was not an easy time. Now the real trouble began. Faced with the authentic love of God, we were immediately engaged in a struggle. But from this time on, Teresa was being loved into the kingdom. She had fundamental doubts about the nature of sexuality and of her own. Fr Louis Matteau and one of the nuns who works with him cared for Sonny. My wife and young son determined that Sonny was to be one of our family and, although separated by space, she is to this day. When it seemed that we might go back to Australia, Sonny wrote and said: "Thank you for making me feel wanted."

There were some beautiful Christian members of our community and without much talk they cared for her and she was eventually received as a full member. Some of our community were Coptic Orthodox Christians from Egypt and they were very afraid for her; the penalty for apostasy in Islam is death. Sonny was tortured by letters from Iran and still fears for the safety of her family and their reaction to her conversion. She was often deeply depressed. In the months that followed Teresa's decision to follow Christ, we shared our hospitality with her, we shared our testimony with her and I always tried to answer her barrage of questions. Jesus of Nazareth, even robbed of his full divinity, is surely one of the most attractive persons. We shared as much as we knew about Jesus — God for us, the Son of God, the second person of the Holy Trinity. We were never ashamed of full-bodied Trinitarianism. We shared our love for God in Christ and for the image and likeness of God in even the most unlovely of our neighbours. The most important thing is that we prayed for Teresa. At this time I was very fortunate in having as my personal assistant a young lady of great efficiency who carried me along. She gave me space to breathe. I was free to pray for three or more hours each day. Sonny's name was often on my lips as I prayed, according to my custom, before the holy icons. Others were faithful in prayer for our new Christian.

A number of Iranians who lived with us thought that Sonny had chosen an easy path of assimilation with a free political asylum at the end. They regarded her attendance at public worship as a betrayal. The Muslims of Arab origin were even more hostile. Sonny can now look back upon a terrible moment of self-doubt. She spoke to God, as she recalls: "Strike me and break my leg if I am not doing this for you. If becoming a Christian is not right." A feeling of peace came over her; she felt "right about it all". Sonny did not know that the strongest opposition did not come from any Muslims. One member of the Christian community and a couple of his hangers-on believed that Sonny was a hypocrite who was using the church. This person made much of Sonny's personal problems. He attacked the spiritual leader of the community for accepting Sonny as a catechumen. The power of the demonic, the very dark side of church life, cannot be known until it has been faced in such a grotesque form of self-righteousness. It was a bitter experience.

Nobody but Teresa can explain the private battle she was fighting. Even now she cannot find the right words for this spiritual warfare. She likens it to schizophrenia. Part of her had made its commitment to Christ. Somebody inside was mocking her. The devil was real to her in this internal spiritual conflict, but more real was Jesus and when she confessed him, in her inmost being, as the Son of God, his peace flowed over her mind and body.

It was obvious that Teresa had to find an expression of Christianity which most suited her: an outward form which corresponded to her inner reality. She has seen more forms of Christian worship than most people. She has been with the writer to highly ritualistic Anglican churches, the

Orthodox church and to the pre-Chalcedonian Orthodox. After a journey of some years she settled for a well-known Anglican charismatic church, though I believe that she is one of those Christians who will always be at home where God's name is truly honoured. Teresa was trained as a Christian where the holy scriptures are revered as they attest to the one word of God. She reads her Bible. She was trained as a sacramental Christian because our Saviour taught us to be such. No way of describing the mystery of the holy eucharist was ever given to her but she accepts the mystery of the true body and precious blood. In her words: "I hate to regard it as just a bit of symbolism."

In June 1981 Sonny Teresa was baptized through the ministry of the writer. At the same service she was confirmed and received the holy gifts from the altar. She was one of two former Muslims who were accepted that day by a bishop in the church of God. They accepted the responsibilities of membership. It was a great occasion for many of us. The angels sang — I believe in angels — and the congregation of every race joined in the praise of the Holy Trinity. It was noticed that the self-appointed judges of the church, mentioned above, broke with the community and stayed away. It was a comment on their wickedness and on the fallen humanity of the broken body of Christ on earth. There is no greater evil than that which calls itself Christian.

When we returned to the house, a group of Muslims held a protest. I attended the meeting as soon as I heard about it. I was allowed to explain that I could become a Muslim if I wished to because we lived in an open society. The meeting broke up. When one of our Muslim brothers left for Arabia some months later he gave me a new copy of the Qur'an and a commentary upon it.

Years have passed. It is always a joy to meet Sonny Teresa. Being a Christian has not been easy for her. She was always told that it would be the way of the cross. She has twice undergone surgery and she has fought even greater inner conflict. But she has been blessed and healed in ways that are beyond understanding. I remember in the early days how she rebelled against mass evangelism in the Albert Hall, but since her baptism she has found great joy in a large congregation, just as she first found it in small groups. In her spiritual life she has also developed. As she says: "I felt a need for the gifts of the Spirit and therefore asked God for the gift of tongues and of healing with any other which God would have for me." God has blessed her faithfulness with his grace in response to this request and used Teresa as an instrument of his peace and healing, bringing others to him. She has been greatly blessed by new leaders and new members in the work of her community.

Teresa is not the only Muslim I have baptized and I am confident in asserting that the way of evangelism in the house of Islam is through a "kenotic" ministry, emptied of self but listening, ready to answer but not speaking first, loving for the sake of him who loved us and praying as if life itself depended on it: like John the Baptist, pointing always to Jesus who is the key to the understanding of God, the universe and humanity.

My Journey

SHIRLEY SHULTZ

I was born in Miami, Florida — a fact that has evoked different responses from people through the years. The usual query has been: "What are you doing in Pennsylvania?" The answer is that my father died when I was a little over five years old. This was the early 1930s, and my mother was unable to support herself and two children and so we moved to Catasauqua, Pennsylvania, to live with her three sisters and one brother. This was my home until I entered nursing school in September 1946.

I don't remember much about my early Christian education, except that a good neighbour took me to the Lutheran church where she taught. I was about 11 or 12 years old when I started attending Salem Evangelical and Reformed church.

My memories of Salem are positive ones. Various family-oriented events (to which I went alone mostly) provided fellowship and good food. Participation in dramatizations at Christmas and Easter made me feel included in the church's life. The church basement was the meeting place for a Tri-Hi-Y Girls' Club which was led by a dedicated church school teacher who later on was also my junior high science instructor and my senior high homeroom teacher. (There were also two other church members whom I had as high school teachers.) This girls' club was my first experience of ecumenism in the church, for membership was not limited to Salem's families or to Protestants. Roughing it at a summer camp in the Poconos was a bonus for being in the club.

As an adolescent, I attended worship services fairly regularly despite the long walk involved, and decided to become confirmed while in the ninth grade. Church was a haven for me. I liked the familiar music and liturgies. They made me feel secure and loved, as I felt very much alone after my favourite aunt died in 1942 and my handsome, popular Marine Corps brother was killed in 1944. I don't think of my teen years as being generally happy ones. I was not part of the crowd that congregated after school hours at an "in" place. A "homeboy", I spent my time studying, reading, listening to the radio or going to the movies or swimming in the summers.

I went into nursing feeling it was the right choice for me. Perhaps it was the influence of my mother's older sister and the experience of having a semi-invalid aunt in the home for several years. I did think that perhaps I could help others. I learned more than just basic nursing skills. A small town girl, I was exposed to city life and to people of other races and faiths. I found myself to be accepting of people for who they were and not what they were as individuals.

After being second in my high school class, I now found I was quite ordinary compared to some of my classmates. At one particularly difficult phase, I wanted to quit, but my mother convinced me that you don't give up when life gets rough, but you persevere and conquer. I did overcome the hurdle of pharmacology, so much so that I can honestly say that I never made an error in medications. I received the highest score in an orientation course years later when I considered re-entering the profession.

While in nursing school, I would return home on free weekends so that I could attend "my" church. If schedules did not allow the necessary travelling time, I would go to other churches near campus. There was always an inner desire and need to be in church on Sundays, or else Sundays were not "right".

As a third-year student, I met my husband-to-be when I joined the course on psychiatric nursing. He was a first-year student attending school on the GI bill. We were married on 1 October 1949, within a week after my finishing school. Throughout that year and the following year, we occasionally attended churches that provided evening services. I worked until June 1950, when my pregnancy made it uncomfortable for me to continue on duty. In August, a month before our son was born, my mother's older sister died. I was not allowed to travel upstate to be with the family and I regretted that. Six weeks after having a caesarean section, I had to have an appendectomy. Our mothers, both of them, came to stay a while in our small furnished apartment to help.

The following spring the baby and I were moved to Danville, Pa., to live with my husband's parents and two sisters in order to escape the summer heat. When he finished his schooling, he joined us in a house we had found to rent.

In the next five years, we had three more children. I managed to work part-time because our families helped with child care. They also helped us financially. I began going to church school with the children, but not as a very faithful member. The children had been baptized at the appropriate times, and I had transferred my membership from Salem to Shiloh E and R Church. But this church was not the same; neither was I. I considered the people hypocritical — so nice on Sunday mornings but gossiping about each other during the week. They seemed more interested in raising money and working on bazaars than caring about others. I was so self-righteous without realizing it.

When my husband received a commission for the Army Nurse Corps in 1957, we moved to a Maryland suburb near Walter Reed Army Medical Center. Although we did get to visit historical places while we were there, I remember those two years more for childhood diseases and influenza, with frequent feelings of isolation and frustration. I had no church affiliation and only another couple of friends.

We moved to Levittown, Pa., in July 1959, and soon after, I felt compelled to find a church. That is the only word I can use to describe that strong inner urge. Somehow I knew that the first Sunday in October was Worldwide Communion Sunday and I had to be in church. Thus God led me to Reformation. At the small gathering of believers that particular evening, I felt like the prodigal in the parable. It was liberating and joyous to be home at last, to know God's forgiving love. I became a covenant member of Reformation in December.

The ensuing years found me involved in different aspects of church life. Whatever tasks I undertook were not done with the purpose of earning points with God; they were understood to be my way of serving others in Christ's name. At times I have tried to resist what God would have me do, but the Spirit persists until I say, "Yes, Lord." Obedience to what I perceive as God's will for me is easy when the task is something I enjoy or see myself having a talent for. When it is an unknown territory that I must explore, I ask, "Why me?" The answer is, "Why not you?" Then I find myself experiencing more spiritual growth. An example was leading a Wednesday morning prayer group which God had me initiate twice during the intervals when we were without a pastor.

Sometimes it has been difficult to balance family responsibilities with church responsibilities. The major part of the past 15 years have been influenced by one son's drug addictions, his criminal activities to support his habits, and subsequent imprisonments. We have suffered with him. These stresses affected my husband's health and made me a distrustful person. We have rejoiced with him at signs of maturity and health. We have been with our other children in their trials and joys. Grandparent-hood has given me innumerable reasons to be thankful and joyful.

I believe that the church is the training ground to prepare people of faith for ministry to others, and that the people of God are to be enablers to one another on their faith journey. I understand that each person is at a different stage in faith development and that we are to be loving, encouraging, accepting, inclusive. I believe in the mutual ministry of clergy and lay people, and I feel strongly that lay people should bear more responsibility in sharing with and assisting the clergy in ministry. I see ministry as serving others in love, as a continuance of Christ's work on earth, and when it really happens, there is a glimpse of God's kingdom. In this calling to ministry, the Holy Spirit is present to guide and to chide, to strengthen and to unite.

When our pastoral leader, the Rev. Al Krass, started a lay theology class in spring 1985, little did I know where it would lead. The Holy Spirit has been with this group, guiding, challenging, enlightening our way. Al has generated an enthusiasm in all of us for Bible study and opened new avenues of study. Since I wasn't trained as a child to ask questions or to think for myself (children should be seen and not heard), I am just learning to formulate questions. I benefit from listening to others, and know that I have much to learn.

Somehow through this class and my hospital chaplaincy work, I have felt directed to the lay ministry. I have been encouraged and affirmed by my peers. I still don't know exactly why, or what God's plan is for me, for I think that there are better gifted people than I. God has blessed me with a sense of humour and good health, the ability to empathize with others in pain and to spark enthusiasm in those who are disheartened. I have some organizational skills. Most of all, I care about people as individuals, as part of God's creation. I think I am weak in creative writing skills and I lack confidence in myself.

With God's help and much prayer, I know these weaknesses will lessen. What I have is a commitment to sharing the love God has given me with others, not only within the community of my brothers and sisters in faith, but also outside the walls of the church building.

The Church Witnesses to Her Own

IOANN SVIRIDOV

Years ago, in the late sixties, during that interminable time of "stagnation" after the short Khrushchev's thaw, when we were young we tried to find out who we were and where we were going.

My friend Alexy was about my own age, and were both pondering over our place in this world (when you are seventeen, you are convinced that you, and only you, can determine your own future). We understood each other perfectly but realized the dissimilarity of our world-outlooks.

I was not yet an Orthodox Christian in the full sense of the word, but rather an idealistic Christian not belonging to any confession. He, a son of technocrats, was a pragmatic materialist. We had long and heated arguments. Our ideas were far from clear, but it looked as if I was becoming more and more Orthodox and my friend more and more pragmatic and secular.

Eternity, in his understanding, was infinity — an unvanishing energy — yet he did not totally reject the existence of God. I suppose it is difficult to believe in non-existence.

Once we happened to visit Vladimir, a small ancient town some two hundred kilometres north-east of Moscow. We liked to explore new places and gain some knowledge of the world. Vladimir is a special place in terms of history and culture. It was founded in the twelfth century, and had lived through many foreign invasions. It has many churches, and even at that time some of them were open; there are old icons and frescoes of Andrei Rublev in the magnificent cathedral, which is of the same age as the town. Nearby there was a park for outdoor parties, with coloured lamps and flags and slogans calling people to work for the bright and joyful future promised by the communist party, which is the "mind, honour and conscience of our epoch".

The inhabitants of the town liked to dance — while a bad orchestra played very loudly. Young people fortified themselves with cheap red wine. At first they were cheerful, but later they became quarrelsome. The brass band began its "work" at the time of divine service in the cathedral. We passed this place of "merriment" feeling deep pain and terror. Only one way was open to us — through the church doors. From the world of wild materialistic pseudo-culture, we entered another and very different world.

Beautiful singing and the reading of the Bible which sounded like music brought clear pictures from the gospel to us. Candles and incense contrasted sharply with the mood and the atmosphere. We were on the verge of tears as it was becoming more and more clear to us that the Lord was alive, that we loved him and had not forgotten him, even as he loved us and had not forgotten us.

We came out of the church, and took a bus to the railway station. We travelled in silence. We bought our tickets, boarded the train and sat speechless all the way to Moscow, where we said good-bye to each other. I saw something new in my friend's eyes. I had not seen this "something" before, and it was like reading my own heart.

Within a week Alexy was baptized; and I had my first confession and received the holy communion.

The Missionary Work of Edith Larbi

JAMES K. AGBEBLEWU

Edith Larbi is a middle-aged woman who came to know Christ in 1966. After ten years of primary education she trained as a computer-operator and was employed by an oil company. She is a member of the Evangelical Presbyterian Church in Ghana.

After her conversion Edith was deeply involved in personal evangelism among her colleagues and church members, particularly among members of the church choir to which she belonged. Not long after, she became involved, together with some other Christians, in a Bible study and a prayer fellowship in her church. Through these gradually many more came to know the Lord.

Having a great passion for souls, Edith resigned her job in 1980 and joined the Maranatha Bible College, Accra, Ghana, as a full-time student. She finished the course in August 1982. After a while she joined the Christian Outreach Fellowship of Ghana (COF), an indigenous inter-denominational missionary society whose aim is to reach out to communities in Ghana that have never heard the gospel. Hitherto evangelism has been pursued mostly by foreign missionary bodies, churches and a few local evangelistic bodies. The COF seeks to identify non-evangelized areas through surveys and then mobilize Ghanaian Christians who feel called to full-time missionary service to offer themselves for service among the unreached communities. Each missionary is to raise his or her own financial support and resources from a local church and friends.

Having joined the COF, Edith started to campaign to secure support for her missionary work from her local congregation and some friends. She hails from an area about 150 miles from the Agave district and her dialect is distinctly different from theirs. But for her deep commitment, Edith would not have chosen to work in this area.

The Agave district is made up of about twenty villages whose total population is about 10,000. The people are traditionally religious and they worship various snake, thunder and river gods. Big trees and anthills of peculiar or spectacular appearance are also worshipped as gods. In addition, ancestral worship, witchcraft and sorcery are common. They belong to various cults, some of which are very hostile towards one another, let alone to Christians. Christianity is generally rejected, although there are a few churches dotted here and there belonging to some mainline and small pentecostal groups.

The people are peasant farmers. They produce beans, cassava and maize; some keep a few cattle and others do seasonal fishing in the lakes and lagoons around the Volta river.

These people may be described as migrants because they go fishing and farming during the rainy season and move out to the urban areas in search of work during the dry period of the year when no useful farming activity can be undertaken. Their holdings are very small, often only a fraction of an acre. The annual rainfall is meagre; so are the harvests. A whole village could be empty and deserted during the dry season.

The people live in community settlements with populations ranging from twenty to three-hundred. These areas are infested with mosquitoes and the tsetse-fly during the rainy season. The soil is poor and life hard. For drinking water they must walk several miles away from the settlement.

In areas such as Agave, the evangelist can be rejected outright when he or she starts talking about God. A cheeky or insulting word or action may be the response on the first occasion. On the other hand, a person may indicate that he or she would want to hear further about this new religion at another time.

Any acceptance or hospitality accorded the missionary may initially be kept secret because people are afraid of opposition from families and friends.

One person contacted may tell another, a relation or a friend, and that way a few people may gather to hear the message. The person-to-person strategy may lead the missionary to the chief or head of the community. If convinced, he may invite the elders to join him as he listens to the new message, and enable him to take a decision.

Personal evangelism through visits to homes, farms, river and market places was the commonest strategy used by Edith during the initial stages of her work. Thus, she would visit people in their homes, and as they went on with their work she would speak to them about the Lord Jesus Christ. This may be when the person is shelling maize or beans or preparing her maize meal in the kitchen.

Personal evangelism is the best method because it assures a measure of privacy. If somebody were to raise an alarm, the whole village could attack you for telling people about a God other than their gods.

When the head of the community and some elders accepted the message, an open-air meeting would be permitted. This would also be possible where the majority of the people were not antagonistic to the gospel. The chief would then order drums to be beaten to announce the presence of the missionary. But such cases are rare.

When the people have gathered the message is given and an altar call made for individuals to come forward and testify. Sometimes such open-air meetings are disrupted by hooligans, mostly young people, or by an organized mob from adherents of some cults.

Edith has become everything for the people — doctor, nurse, provider of food, clothing, cooking utensils, etc. She solicits the help of churches and Christians to donate these items, as well as medicines and the things she needs to give first-aid to people in case of minor illnesses and accidents.

Edith believed in the power of prayer to heal. The first convert at Klonu, the first village she went to, was one who was thus healed. Akpalu was a sixty-year old fetish priestess. She was unconscious for days and was brought to Edith to be prayed for. She was supposed to have offended her gods who now wanted to kill her. For five days the old woman lay motionless without taking food or water. It was a challenge to Edith's faith. She struggled in prayer, and the old woman regained consciousness. When she recovered, Akpalu denounced her gods and destroyed all her fetish objects.

Funeral celebrations are very important in Ghanaian culture. People will gather in a village from surrounding villages and from the urban areas, particularly when the deceased is an elder or a popular leader. Edith has been using funeral celebrations to propagate the gospel. In April 1985 a grand funeral was organized for the chief of Klonu. Edith invited members of the Volta Evangelistic Association, of which she is a member, to help with the funeral-related celebration. A vigil was kept, drumming and dancing, by the Christians; they used the traditional musical rhythms of dirges to present the gospel, and the people were amazed by the way their traditional music was Christianized. The Christians stole the show, and many people gathered round them. During the night, a filmstrip was shown and the gospel preached to the crowd.

Quite a few people were won to Christ that night. The next day, the visiting Christians filed past the body to pay their last homage. They were allowed to give a message. The chiefs and elders from other villages who listened to the message later invited Edith to preach the gospel in some of their villages.

Once a converted former fetish priestess was sick and brought to Accra, the capital, for medical treatment. She died in June 1986. When the body was taken to her village, her parents and the chiefs of the village were afraid that the gods would be annoyed because of her conversion to Christianity, and that they might take revenge by killing more people. They did not want the body to be taken into the village. Eventually the elders allowed the body to be brought in. The dead body was beautifully laid out. Nothing like this had ever been seen in the village. The joy, pomp and pageantry which characterized the funeral made both parents give up their idolatry and profess Christ. The body was buried on a piece of farm land offered by a Christian brother, because the chiefs refused burial in the public cemetery.

Other occasions on which cultural performances are used to propagate the gospel include traditional farming (yam) festivals, enthronements, anniversaries of chiefs and durbars of chiefs and people.

In some villages, churches such as the Catholic and the Presbyterian churches had been established many years back. Some of these have small congregations, sometimes fewer than ten. They often become a laughing-stock in the village and their members are looked down upon. Occasionally Edith is invited to preach in them, or she invites herself. Her preaching often sounds like "a new teaching with authority". At the end of the service, the sick are prayed for, with instant healing taking place at times. As a result, many more villagers are drawn to the church, thus starting a revival. Bible study and prayer meetings are organized, and gradually the gospel is accepted by the people.

Churches have been established in 13 villages that have been reached through Edith's work. These churches started sometimes with one or two persons who were illiterate or had only a few years of formal education — such people are the nucleus of a church. Edith worked hard on training them so that in her absence they could act as catechists or leaders. Because of her relationship with the church and the congregations established, Edith has also become catechist-designate to some of the congregations, in addition to being a missionary.

Since a non-denominational congregation does not appeal to some people, Edith has named some of the fellowships after the Evangelical Presbyterian Church, a mother church.

In recognition of Edith's work, the Evangelical Presbyterian Church headquarters offered her a gift of fishing nets and an outboard motor. These are used to give employment to some of the peasants and also to ferry her across the rivers, lagoons and flooded areas during the rainy season. Before then, Edith had to hire boatmen to take her. She also had to hire canoe men to fetch her drinking water from fresh-water rivers many miles away.

The Lord has been gracious to Edith, protecting her from all spiritual and physical attacks by the people opposed to her. No ordinary person could have withstood spiritual assaults through jujus, spells, witchcraft, and all the evil practices of some of the local cults that are known for their deadly power. Lightning may strike, a swarm of bees or an army of scorpions may sting you to death if you openly challenge their gods. Apart from such wicked spiritual attacks, the people can physically attack you when you are travelling alone, or they may even throw you into the river when ferrying you across. In all these, God has been Edith's fortress and shield.

One characteristic that has impressed people is Edith's social and cultural adaptability. She has learned the accent of the people's language and can articulate her message in such a way that her listeners hear her speak in their own dialect. Edith will mingle with all kinds of people, male and female, young and old, and join them in their activities, domestic and vocational. Edith will have a smile for you even when you reject her. No matter how much she is provoked, she remains calm. All this has led people to Christ; they see the love of Jesus plainly in Edith's life.

Some of the young people, and even the old converts of Edith, have been severely persecuted by their non-believing families and other villagers. Younger people have been thrown out of their homes. Some have been denied food, schooling and parental care, and some have been beaten physically by relations and friends. Edith has had to shelter and feed some of them overnight, and sometimes for days and weeks. The persevering and faithful among them have survived these persecutions. In some cases, young people ostracized by their families have been taken out of the villages and given to the care of Christians in other places.

Miss Edith Larbi is the first woman missionary working among her own people in Ghana. She is a totally committed Christian, doing pioneering missionary work among her people.

The Roots of Life

HAGOP DINGILIAN

My journey may be said to have started with my mother who is an orphan of the Armenian genocide. She was a year old when both her parents were massacred. She grew up in an American orphanage and eventually came to Alexandria, Egypt, where she was married and I was born and raised.

I received my first understanding of Armenian culture from my mother; as I started going to school my circle of friends expanded and so did my understanding of culture. But within a short period of time, I noticed that there was something different about me. I seemed to take everything too seriously.

I was neither happy nor able to laugh whole-heartedly like other children. They always seemed to be carefree, whereas I tended to worry about things. Even at that early stage I used to think about the meaning of life and the mystery of death. Particularly disturbing for me were discussions that dealt with the Armenian genocide and the question of who belonged to the Armenian nation. There was more to life than these topics and it was pointless to waste my life discussing these issues. I would get nervous and angry if these issues were forced upon me.

Consequently, I felt relieved when the whole family moved to the United States in 1969. First, I was going from a very traditional, conservative Middle Eastern culture where you spoke only when you were spoken to, to a very open, liberal Western culture where you had to speak out just to survive. Second, I was leaving behind all those issues that revolved round the vicissitudes of the Armenian nation and the genocide.

I could now bury my past and look forward to the future!

In the north-eastern parts of the United States I went to school, received my bachelor of science degree in chemical engineering and started work as a chemical engineer in one of the major corporations in the United States. At the age of twenty, I seemed to have all the comforts that a young man could want, except friendship! Everyone around me seemed to be having a good time at parties, going to restaurants and bars, going on nature hikes... in short, enjoying life, while I was still worried, preoccupied, and not able to shake off those worries about life and death.

I started falling ill for weeks and months at a time. I thought perhaps I could not adjust to the colder climate and I needed to be in a warmer climate similar to that of my birthplace. So I moved to Los Angeles, California, nine years after coming to the United States. Without my conscious knowledge this was my first move back to my roots.

You would not believe the joy and the relief I felt when I saw the palm trees and the beaches for the first time. It was like a dream come true. I resumed my career as a chemical engineer, helped the rest of the family move to California, bought a new car and a house, and seemed to have everything in life a man could want — everything except... a soul mate. So I started looking for one, but I found it difficult to make any promises to a woman, especially when these had to do with a life commitment.

Living was just too serious to take tomorrow lightly. Death could cut it short any time without any notice, and turn a long-term commitment into a huge lie.

Perhaps I thought I needed to enter the Armenian community where people speak the same language, eat the same kind of food as I do and share the same national history as I do. Without my knowing, this was one more step closer to my roots. The novelty of speaking Armenian, the smell of shish-kebab and the taste of baklava were beyond this world... at least for a year or so! However, when it came to making a personal commitment, I was as scared as ever. If someone got close to me, I would try to run away and, when that did not work, I would become nervous and angry. I could not love and I would not allow myself to be loved! I was sad, full of self-pity, angry and finally depressed. Everything around me seemed to be devoid of life, and there was no meaning to life. Death was inevitable, regardless of how one lived. And worse, life in this world seemed to be full of deception and violence and chaos and suffering. Life was not worth living. There was no way out except suicide!

And then I heard a voice: "Be of good cheer, I have overcome the world." I cannot explain it, but with that somehow everything made sense. Someone, Jesus Christ, had conquered death. God is the God of the living, not of the dead.

I was returning to my roots. I had to go and become a priest in the Armenian Apostolic Church. I left everything behind and went to the seminary of the Armenian Church in New York. I did not know why I was there, but I knew there was a reason. During the first semester at the seminary there was a course where we would discuss the Armenian genocide. After 32 years, I was certainly tired of hearing about this issue. But out of a sense of duty I started reading one of the required books where eyewitness accounts of the genocide were given by both Armenians and non-Armenians. Reading the book, tears started flowing from my eyes. I kept reading for days — crying, weeping, panting, gasping — but I could not put the book down! I did not come out of the room for days. I was not present at the genocide but the genocide was present in me! I felt sad, then self-pity set in, then frustration and finally anger. Isn't there anything other than death and dying in this world? What kind of people are those who carry out such barbaric acts? What kind of a God is he who allows all this to happen?

And then I heard a voice: "I am the way and the truth and the life." There was total silence and peace. Yes, there is a way to live in peace — and that is the life with Jesus Christ: "In me you have peace... in this world you have tribulation." Yes, there is life which needs to be faced, and one can face it with Christ: "You shall know the truth, and the truth shall set you free." And yes, there is a reason to live and a reason to die — one simply needs to know Jesus Christ and follow him; he is the giver of life and he is life.

First, I had to be cleansed of the sin of anger and pride. I needed personally to know God and the Christ whom he sent to free humankind from all the evil in this world. I needed to turn the destructive anger in me into a loving life-giving spirit and a new way of life. I needed to overcome the pride which led to self-pity. This was not just my suffering — but it was the suffering of the whole Armenian nation, and even of other nations of the world as well, Jews in Nazi Germany, the people of Cambodia and now in Ethiopia. A step closer to my roots. This prayer of the Armenian Catholicos St. Nersess Shnorhali from the twelfth century was a great help:

All Merciful Lord,
Have mercy upon all who believe in You,
Ours and those of other nations,
Those whom I know and those whom I don't,
Those who are alive and those who have passed away,
And pardon my enemies
And those who hate me
For the crimes they have committed against me,
And turn them back from the evil deeds that

they have planned against me,
So that they may be worthy of your mercy.
And have mercy upon your creatures;
And upon me a manifold sinner.

Second, I needed to find out the truth. So the following summer when I went back to Los Angeles, as I took my mother to church Sunday after Sunday, while driving for an hour and a half, I used to listen to her recounting what she had heard of the genocide and how she felt and what she experienced afterwards as she was growing up. Talking of her experiences, she used to cry without stopping. I tried to comfort her... but could not. I had not prayed and meditated enough about this situation myself. I started falling ill again, feeling dizzy, having stomach pains and headaches.

And then I read: "Your sins are forgiven. Rise, take up your pallet and walk." Jesus Christ, the source of life himself, healed me. So at Christ's command I picked up my pallet, the truth that I learned about my life and my nation's history, and started walking forward in life. It was a long awaited trip — one from the depths of hell and death to the heights of heaven and eternal life. It was a trip back to my spiritual roots. Through Jesus Christ I was at peace within my own being and was able to face the truth and know my national heritage.

But there was one more question left: "'Our God', 'Our God', why did you forsake us?" Why did God allow all this to happen to us? This was not a simple issue of just accepting or forgiving and forgetting. That is no way to live, especially for a Christian. Not only did I need to understand "why", but I was given the task to explain it to others as well, those around me and those far away, those who are Armenian and those who are not.

And then a voice came: "Truly, truly, I say to you, unless a grain of wheat falls to the ground and dies, it remains alone; but if it dies, it bears much fruit."

We, the Armenians, were the first nation to accept Christianity as our official faith in 301 A.D. Christ himself came down and established our church. Our alphabet was given by God. Our literature, art and architecture came through the church. Our whole concept of nationhood and culture, the way of life in this world, was based on the life and the teachings of Christ, on our loving God and others. For these reasons it had to be the Armenians who had to be the chosen people, to be worthy to carry the cross as a nation for their salvation and that of other nations.

We Armenians have suffered through the centuries for our faith and continue to do so, yet we remain faithful to Christ, so that as St Gregory the Illuminator stated in the midst of his suffering: "This patience in the face of suffering is for God to see, O pagan king, how strong is my love for him, and for you to see that no extent of earthly suffering could separate me from the love of my Lord, Jesus Christ." This is to show all, that through all the suffering in this world, people and nations can come to Christ and only to Christ, the source of life, to be healed, and have eternal life in God's kingdom.

Now I could go to Armenia to get even closer to my roots. I was ordained in the mother see of Etchmiadzin. I preach, teach in the seminary and other educational institutions, and minister to the sick. I am always busy in the Lord's service as Armenia awakens to a new life from the long sleep of seventy years and rediscovers her own roots of faith and history. I was married to a young lady from Armenia. I can now live among my people, face the anxieties and frustrations as they do, such as the Sumgait massacre where Azerbaijanis killed many Armenians (just ten weeks after our devastating 1988 earthquake), the continuous border skirmishes and funeral processions for those killed there, the blockade of Armenia, lack of gas, heat, bread and sometimes even water.

I can now face all these because I am rooted in God and in my national heritage. In the face of all the difficulties of life, I can love and I can allow myself to be loved, I can be at peace and never lose faith.

The Armenian nation can do the same as well. One nation attempted to annihilate another — but failed and failed miserably! This is to show that nationhood just as personhood is given by God and no nation can annihilate a God-believing nation just as one person cannot annihilate another person. The body they may kill, but the spirit belongs to God and no one can touch it.

Any nation that attempts to annihilate a people whose life is centred in Christ and his teachings, or tries to suppress their history, is attempting to defeat the purposes of God. It is God who will judge them!

Now I have returned to my spiritual and physical roots. Instead of frustration and anger, mercy and compassion filled my heart towards all who had directly taken part in the massacres and those who stood by and did nothing as one and a half million Armenians were slaughtered.

These people are not the enemies of the Armenians because they are already dead! Rather the enemy of the Armenians and of all nations is the Deceiver of the people and those who follow this Deceiver are truly the people who need to be pitied most, for they don't understand the meaning of life and love. Here is a "Prayer for the Nations" that I wrote:

All-loving Father, forgive them for
they do not know what they do.
In vain they persecute us,
For mindless gains they abuse us,
and when all that's left are our dead bodies...
even then they continue to torture us.
Now O Lord, it is the cross we have to climb,
We are ready!
Our blood we need to shed for you,
We are ready!
Since we know that you are the one who established us,
We are ready!
Since you promised salvation for us from the beginning,
We are ready!
Since you are the One who was, who is, and who is to come,
We are ready!
New Jerusalem we await in hope,
Coming down from heaven, adorned as a bride,
For living your promised eternal life
we look forward to share,
With our sister nations from all races and faiths,
With you as the only All Holy Trinity,
The Father and the Son and the Holy Spirit,
now and always and unto ages of ages.
Amen!

Seek not Healing but Christ

THEODORE H. PERERA

Dev Suwa Sevawa is Sinhalese for home of healing, a ministry where those who are sick in body, mind and spirit receive intensive prayer care as well as medical help. At the regular healing services attended by Buddhists, Hindus, Muslims and Christians, the gospel call is "don't seek healing, seek the Lord Jesus Christ".

Tissa, a middle-aged Buddhist, was one such who came seeking healing. Dressed in an immaculate white "national dress", wearing dark glasses and carrying flowers, he was led into my room at Dev Suwa Sevawa. He was blind.

"I am a practising Buddhist," began Tissa. "I seek restoration of sight without changing religion. These flowers are an offering."

"We do not offer flowers, but we can place them on the altar, in vases," I responded, accepting his gift.

Tissa, satisfied and relaxed, sat on a chair beaming. "How long have you been blind?" I asked him. "For four years," he replied. "I was retired prematurely from government service. Eye surgeons ruled out operation, saying I would be blind for life."

"How did you happen to come here?" "It is a long story. I should not take your time."

"I'm interested. Please go on."

Thus assured, Tissa cleared his throat and began: "I longed for sight and hoped that something would happen. Recently, when my wife was clearing her shopping bag, her eyes fell on a healing story printed on some wrapping paper which was a sheet out of a religious magazine. Impressed by it, she read it to me. It was an amazing story about a Chinese Buddhist girl who lived in America. Her mother was seriously ill and one day, in desperation, she had prayed: 'Jesus, can you hear me? My mother is dying. I heard over the radio a preacher say that you are the living Lord Jesus who heals. So please heal my mother. I want her.' In a moment her mother had sat up, healed and restored. They had later become Christians. This story impressed me and later I related it to a visiting cousin and remarked that if Jesus heals like that in Sri Lanka, I could have my sight again. He then took me by surprise, saying 'Jesus heals today in Sri Lanka'."

"'How do you know? You too are a Buddhist.' 'Haven't you heard how my sister was healed?' 'Wasn't she operated on?' 'Yes, she was. We were all standing outside the operating theatre, when a doctor came out and announced that she was bleeding and that they were unable to arrest it, and that she could die if the blood did not coagulate. We yelled out in grief.

"Just then a woman came there and on hearing what had happened, told us: "Don't wait here crying as if she is dead. Jesus can heal her. Get into a car and go to Dev Suwa Sevawa. They will pray with you and your sister will be healed." We rushed to Moratuwa — 18 kilometres away. Father Theodore prayed with us and told us how when Jesus said the word, the sick person who was far away was healed at the very instant. He further said: "Go in faith, and Jesus will do likewise for your sister." We left Dev Suwa Sevawa at 7.30 p.m. and got to the hospital to find that the bleeding had stopped exactly at seven thirty.'

"I believed it when she said that Jesus healed her sister. So I made enquiries about Dev Suwa Sevawa and longed to come here. Some time later my friend, who has brought me here today, visited me. He is a Roman Catholic, and he knew about your ministry; his son had been healed here and he had your two books which he lent to us. My wife has read them to me and my hope in Jesus has been strengthened and I am seeking restoration of my sight."

I listened to Tissa with rapt attention and said: "God has indeed spoken to you in signs. Don't seek healing, seek the Lord Jesus Christ."

I talked to him about Jesus to build up his faith and to bring him to the foot of the cross for healing. He was in a state of expectancy. Minutes later, he knelt very fervently at the altar and waited before God in supplication as I touched his eyes and prayed to Jesus to restore his sight. Tissa went away a happy man.

A month later he came back beaming, and said: "Something is happening to me. I can see streaks of light." We were thrilled and we praised God then and there and prayed for full healing. We also continued to pray for him in our daily prayer cells with thanksgiving.

After another month he reported further improvement: "I have peace within me, though I don't see as yet. The streaks of light continue to appear."

Over a period of five months, Tissa matured in spiritual stature. He trusted in Jesus for a miracle and talked of it hopefully and with certainty.

After six months of prayer I urged Tissa to visit his former eye surgeon, saying: "Go in faith and show yourself to the surgeon." Tissa was surprised and unwilling to do that. "God uses surgeons as his instruments. Now's the time to consult," I advised.

Some time later Tissa went to the eye surgeon who, after examination, had expressed surprise at the dramatic change and asked him what he had done. Tissa said: "I have been praying to Jesus to heal my eyes."

We rejoiced that this our Buddhist patient witnessed to his Buddhist doctor that he is trusting in Jesus for restoration of his sight.

The doctor now suggested an operation. Tissa agreed only after much persuasion from us. We waited in prayer precisely at the hour of the operation and it turned out to be a success.

Two months later Tissa himself wrote to me saying: "I can now see. This is the first letter I have written since my sight was restored. I will come to give thanks to Jesus. I long to see your face which I have not yet seen."

Soon after, Tissa came and stood before me saying: "How happy I am to see your face at long last." I was inspired to reply: "Yes, with your sight restored you now see my face, whereas previously without sight you saw Jesus."

We knelt together to praise and give thanks to God. Tissa kept in touch with us and sent a thank-offering annually as from "a grateful Buddhist pilgrim", remembering the day his eyes were opened. He witnessed to many that Jesus healed him, but remained a Buddhist. When he died in May 1985, his wife informed us that according to his wishes, his eyes were donated and two people, who had his cornea grafted to their blind eyes, now see. This is a matter of great merit to the dead, according to Tissa's widow. To us it is a matter of great importance that the testimony lives on.

If we had any sadness that Tissa remained a Buddhist, then it could be claimed that we had great joy when Lou, a high government official, and his family were baptized on Easter Sunday 1975. It is wonderful how the Lord draws people. Lou once reprimanded Ernest, a lethargic subordinate officer, who then pleaded, in excuse, tiredness due to strain and stress of work. That evening Ernest, smarting under the reprimand, felt even more exhausted and broken, and was walking home dejected. A friend, Richard, met him and on being told what took place that day, he exhorted

Ernest to attend a healing service at Dev Suwa Sevawa which was close to his home.

Accepting this chance meeting as providential, Ernest came here and found Jesus. The following Sunday he went to church after twenty years and kept coming to our healing services.

Lou was quick to notice the change and complimented Ernest. Thereupon Ernest told Lou of all that took place. "Something wonderful happened. I found Jesus there and he has turned me around and I am healed in body, mind and spirit. I do more work than ever before."

Lou was delighted and interested, specially about his meeting Jesus, and asked Ernest: "Where is this Dev Suwa Sevawa?"

So Ernest brought Lou and his wife Wimala to our healing service. Though Buddhists, they knelt in deep adoration and entered very fervently into the spirit of the prayer that was offered and the Lord placed his hand upon Lou's right shoulder. Lou witnessed later:

"When I first heard of the healing ministry of Father Theodore, I was not ill in body. Yet my mind and spirit were restless in the search for truth and righteousness. So, one Tuesday evening, I joined Ernest, my colleague, to go to Dev Suwa Sevawa. We entered a small but impressive church by a lake. It was peaceful and tranquil within, and was conducive to my own search. I was impressed by the extreme simplicity of the service, which commenced with a strong and stirring prayer by Father Theodore: 'The Lord is in his holy temple, let the whole creation be still before him.' We instinctively moved into a state of devotion. 'The Lord God saith: Be still and know that I am God.' We entered into a holy silence and I felt a touch on my right shoulder, and I turned my head sideways. There was no hand on my shoulder and it was a mystery. Soon I realized that the Lord Jesus Christ was present at this healing service. The testimonies of those healed corroborate the bold declaration of Father Theodore that the Lord Jesus was at work performing miracles in Sri Lanka. And now I believe it, for Jesus touched me and healed me in body, mind and spirit."

From then on this family came regularly and it was quite evident that Lou was being drawn to Jesus. He read the Bible and asked questions, and committed himself to Jesus. Every morning on his way to the office, he worshipped at the Colombo Fort YMCA Chapel. After a few months he asked for baptism. I waited until his wife too resolved to follow Jesus. Shortly thereafter their son Gehan also accepted Jesus as his Saviour.

Thus on Easter morning I baptized Wimala and three other Buddhist women converts in the church; and Lou, Gehan, two other Buddhist men converts and two Hindu men converts in the river.

Lou further testified: "Since Jesus touched me I have received baptism along with my wife and teenage son and I have drawn many persons to Dev Suwa Sevawa to witness the glory of the risen Lord. We are now pilgrims on the road walking with the Lord. He heals, restores and reconciles, and is infinite in love."

One day, on an official visit to Baddegama, Lou met Gamage, a Buddhist, who looked sad and troubled. Gamage told Lou: "My wife had breast cancer and since the mastectomy she lives in constant fear of pain. Her depression, aggravated by women office-mates' chatter, is adversely affecting our lives. To make matters worse, though we have been married for twelve years, she is childless. So she has lost the desire to live."

Straight away Lou had witnessed: "The Lord Jesus can help you in your distress. Take her to Moratuwa to the Dev Suwa Sevawa healing service." And so Gamage contacted a Christian friend who, together with Rev. Bhareti, the Anglican priest of Baddegama, brought her here for ministration.

Eight months later Rev. Bhareti wrote to me: "Praise God for answered prayers. Mrs Gamage has had a double cure. I remember how you spoke to them of Jesus, saying: 'Seek Jesus who heals. Accept your healing now as we pray for you. Go in faith. Start working tomorrow itself.' Together we then prayed with laying-on-of hands. You also prayed that she may conceive and bring forth a child. I met Gamage recently. His wife has recovered fully and is seven months pregnant. How wonderful! People say it is a miracle." Mrs Gamage gave birth to a healthy baby. Mother and child were doing well when last we heard of them.

Samanthi, a Buddhist girl of 12 years passed away peacefully to be with Jesus whom she loved. She was the eldest of seven children born into a peasant family of Katiyawa, a remote village in the dry zone of Sri Lanka. Following several years of inadequate rain, Richard, her father, had no water for his rice fields. He eked out a living by dry cultivation. Samanthi's family lived in a wattle and daub hut in abject poverty. To add to the misery of it all, Samanthi had a congenital heart defect and lay on a mat, dying.

Richard, inconsolable and desperate, wrote to the newspapers enquiring where he could take her for healing. The response was tremendous — 628 replies.

The villagers helped him to read and categorize these letters. They found a letter written by one Swinitha of Moratuwa, saying: "Jesus heals today. No money is needed to obtain divine healing. Bring your child to Dev Suwa Sevawa. Jesus will heal her."

Richard, after some consultation, decided to act on this letter. He wrote to Swinitha and informed her that he would bring the girl to Dev Suwa Sevawa.

Richard mortgaged the expected harvest of rice to obtain money for travel expenses and set out early one morning, carrying in his arms his weak, emaciated daughter; he walked three miles through the fields to board a bus to Colombo — a distance of two-hundred miles. As the child was very ill, people vacated the rear bench of the bus so that she might lie on it. Exhausted, she fell asleep. Enquiring passengers obtained from Richard details of the illness and the purpose of the journey. Already he was talking about Jesus.

It turned out to be a rainy day. Their bus was held up for many hours because of flood waters and fallen trees. It was night when they reached Colombo. In heavy rain and with the child on his shoulder, Richard crossed the road and heard the screeching of brakes which jolted him. A car narrowly missed him. He was terrified. But the driver had compassion. He got out and when he saw the child, he recognized her. He said: "Get into my car. I am the doctor who treated your child at the Anuradhapura hospital." That was providential. The good Samaritan first took them to his home and fed them. Since the child was very ill, he had her admitted to the children's hospital that very night.

The next day Richard came to Dev Suwa Sevawa with Swinitha and at our healing service the whole congregation prayed very earnestly for Samanthi's healing.

A couple of days later, something wonderful happened. Samanthi made a miraculous recovery. On the following Tuesday, at our healing service, people praised God when she stood up beside me. For two years thereafter she stayed out of hospital and her health improved daily.

Samanthi was keen to learn of Jesus who had healed her, and corresponded with us. Soon, through Samanthi, her whole family accepted Jesus as their Lord and Saviour. On Richard's invitation, we visited them and conducted a healing service in their village. A large crowd heard with gladness the gospel message that Jesus heals today. Richard testified. Samanthi, of course, was a living testimony. Their baptism was postponed for the want of a Bible teacher. Then one night Samanthi woke up saying Jesus had appeared to her and beckoned her to

Dev Suwa Sevawa to receive full healing. She insisted that they go at once, but Richard had to find the money. Four days later they set out and once again it was night when they reached Colombo.

Samanthi complained of a severe chest pain. She was rushed to hospital and there she died. Richard took her body home for burial.

A party of us from Dev Suwa Sevawa visited them within the week and Richard told us that he did not bury her according to Buddhist rites. In fact, for want of a Christian priest or layman, he himself had committed her body to the grave and her soul to the Lord Jesus. We were greatly encouraged to see their faith had not been shaken and we had a prayer meeting beside her grave.

Before we left, Richard asked for baptism. So a month later we got Richard, his wife and the six children down to Dev Suwa Sevawa and in the presence of a very large gathering, Richard testified, moving people to tears.

Thereafter, they affirmed their belief in Jesus, and I baptized them, and they remain faithful to God and live among their people as witnesses of Christ.

Young Black Londoners

GRAHAM KINGS

The brick hit the wall above the youth club door and dropped, broken, on to the floor. The neat notch out of the plaster, ten inches from where my head had been, would need to be explained to the congregation.

Then a metal bracket, flung at short range, landed with a thud in the back of one of our black youth workers. He ran outside, grabbed the young West Indian who had thrown it, and beat him up. Hardly non-directive counselling, but very effective!

Later we chatted over our reactions to this violence of gatecrashers, who were above the age limit, and also the question of turning the other back. Then the youth worker had slipped off home, via the back door, to avoid revenge on revenge.

Our Thursday evening open youth club for 11s to 15s was not always that exciting, but was rarely peaceful. Roller skating/dancing demanded speed, precision and daring swerves to avoid younger members. Carl and Desmond were particularly brilliant at it. Des felt at home in the church hall, since he had been there in various Sunday school groups; but when Carl skated in one Thursday, it was something else. He, his mother, his sister and grandmother had recently moved into a house just up the road from the church.

We had our fair share of hassles with members over broken record players, stolen sweets and sweet-smelling cigarettes (!), but also amazing fun with a sponge football, bar football, pool table and table tennis. For several weeks, some brought their own sound system, set it up in the choir vestry, and had "toasting" competitions: this involved spontaneous, amplified, singing over recorded, rhythmic, backing music.

The aim of the club was to help young people in our community realize that they mattered to God, because they mattered to us. Many felt they had been thrown on the rubbish heap of British society; but we believed that God does not throw things or people away — he mends them. Most members had no direct involvement in the church, but the fascinating network of relatives and friends meant that they often knew people in the congregation. There was no epilogue; emphasis was rather put on building personal relationships, and gradually these led to interesting questions being asked.

A weekend away, subsidized by the church, was organized to allow more time for these relationships and questions. We stayed in a small Methodist church hall at Leigh-on-Sea, about an hour's drive east of London. There were three boys and three girls plus four leaders, one of whom was Les Isaac, a young black evangelist and great friend of mine. Carl came, but Des could not make it.

We had great fun with races on the beach, eating fresh shrimps and cockles, and discussions late into the night. We listened, fascinated, to the story of Les's life. He had had a violent youth: by the age of 13 he had been leading gangs in street battles against white skinheads in North London. Then at 17 he became a serious Rastafarian[1] with long dreadlocks, spending his time smoking ganja (cannabis) and sitting around reasoning from the Bible. His world was shattered in 1974 when he saw his Messiah and God, Haile Selassie, on the news at ten ignoring the poor in Ethiopia. Soon after that a friend, who had recently become a Christian, spoke to him in the street and one night in his room he knelt down and decided to be a follower of Jesus, who really was good news to the poor. That night he cut his dreadlocks, and hurled his valuable ganja right out of the window. Since then he has been going round youth clubs in his spare time, sharing this good news.

The most startling experience of the weekend for me was going swimming in the nearby indoor pool. As we walked out together from the changing rooms, everyone stopped and stared at us; it was extraordinary. They had obviously never seen black people close up before, and we all felt the force of their stares. It struck me for the first time that my life really was bound up with these young people. We enjoyed fooling around in the pool and on the way back, and late into the night, we explored these feelings of being stared at and of being black in a white society.

---

[1] Rastafarianism originated in Jamaica in 1930. Its roots lie in the experience of slavery, poverty, racism and a deep longing to return to Africa. In the 1920s Marcus Garvey, a Jamaican political activist, had proclaimed "Look to Africa when a black king shall be crowned, for the day of deliverance is near." In 1930 Ras Tafari (Prince Tafari) was crowned Emperor Haile Selassie of Ethiopia, with the titles "lord of lords" and "king of kings". Basic beliefs include the divinity of Selassie, God's judgment on white society (the "Babylon" of the Bible), and a return of black people to Africa (especially Ethiopia).

Over that weekend, Carl felt he wanted to follow Les's example in following Jesus and he prayed a prayer of commitment, written at the back of an evangelistic booklet.

Lord Jesus Christ,
I know I have sinned in my thoughts, words and actions.
There are so many good things I have not done.
There are so many sinful things I have done.
I am sorry for my sins and turn from everything I know to be wrong.
You gave your life upon the cross for me.
Gratefully I give my life back to you.
Now I ask you to come into my life.
Come in as my Saviour and cleanse me.
Come in as my Lord to control me.
Come in as my Friend to be with me.
And I will serve you all the remaining years of my life
in complete obedience. Amen.

He was thrilled and soon wanted everybody to know about it.

We returned home and the next week Carl brought Des round to our house. He said: "Des doesn't believe that just saying a little prayer written in a booklet makes you a Christian." I was soon to learn that there was some truth in Des's comment; the process of conversion was more complicated than I had realized.

It was not just a matter of Christ coming into his life, but also of Carl being transferred into Christ's life. Day-to-day feelings and decisions about truth and lies, peace and violence, hope and fear, love and hate, proceeded in fits and starts. Sometimes there was one step backwards and two forwards; sometimes vice versa! I came to recognize that there would be many turnings and returnings in his life. Des could see, however, that something had clearly happened to Carl, and his friends at school were talking about the change in his life. Carl had also shown the booklet to his mum, gran and sister; they had all prayed the little prayer and his sister wanted to join a Sunday school group.

This was the first of many weekly meetings on Fridays after school, with tea and toast. The three of us, and sometimes another friend from school, would talk through various things that had happened in the week, together with other things on their minds, and we would look at relevant passages in the Bible. We talked about being stopped by the police at random, and being searched, about their bleak job prospects in spite of a cheery careers advisory officer, and about violence in the home. Usually we would end up discussing God and sex, or God and ganja!

God changed me through these times together. I found new gut-level ways of praying and many new biblical angles on issues. As we looked at Jesus' radical attitude to the Samaritans and Paul's crucial theme of Jews and Gentiles united in Christ, I was horrified to discover racism in myself and in my background. Carl and Des would often come up with a bright idea that shed light on their own questions. When I had difficulty explaining the different sorts of churches in our community, Carl said: "They're like packets of crisps aren't they? Many different flavours — but they're all crisps."

St Mark's Harlesden is a multi-racial church, roughly half black and half white, and the worship to me seemed lively; but for them it was pretty boring and they were regularly irregular. The question of Carl's hat became an interesting flashpoint. Some members of the congregation, both black and white, felt affronted (on God's behalf, of course) that he refused to take his hat off in church. Unfortunately I never summoned up the courage to comment that bishops usually wore hats in church!

One Sunday, soon after the weekend away, there was a baptism and Carl and Des rushed to the front to get a closer look at exactly what was going on. The worried sidesman quickly encouraged them back to their seats. However, the vicar and many in the church had been praying hard for the youth club for some time; they realized that a church which prays for new people is inevitably challenged to change, by the very answers to their prayers. A plan to carpet the church hall was scrapped because it would have meant banning football on Thursday evenings.

Gradually, after a year or so, the Friday sessions after school also became irregular. Carl and Des continued coming to the club for a while, till they passed the age limit. Then Des left his mother and stepfather and went to live with his father in Birmingham; and Carl, his mum and sister had to move out of his gran's house. I never saw Des again but after some time, and feeling a bit of a failure, I managed to trace Carl and his family through the social services, just before I finished working in the parish.

They were living in two cramped rooms in a hotel used for council accommodation. Carl no longer went to church, or prayed that much, but asked after Les and our family. I said we had had a second daughter and were leaving to work in East Africa; Les had got married — to a careers advisory officer — and has just written a book about his life as a Rastaman and his conversion. He then dragged me off to see a friend of his in another room, who had recently become a Christian and who was enthusing about his new faith.

I left Carl with a promise and a prayer: a promise to send him a signed copy of Les's book; and a prayer that God would continue to bring people into his life, like his new friend, who would challenge him with the exciting reality of God's kingdom.

Oases of Spiritual Life and Witness

IVAN TSELEV DIMITROV

It was a pleasant autumn day in 1989, a little before the "autumnal spring" in the political, social and spiritual life of our country. A friend and colleague had invited me to deputize for him as cantor at the Sunday divine liturgy at the convent of the Dormition of the Mother of God, a few kilometres outside Sofia.

The convent is situated on Mount Vitosa, above the village of Drangalevski, a suburb of the capital. The nuns are few and aged. Despite their zeal, hard work and willingness, they cannot meet all the needs of the convent. So, among other things, for all the Sunday services and all the festive ceremonies, they have recourse to the services of an outside cantor. Fortunately, there is a permanent rector, a man of kind disposition, diligent and very amiable.

On every Sunday and feast day the convent church is full to bursting with pious folk from the capital. The worshippers normally come with their families, to pray at the divine liturgy and to take the holy communion; babies, children, young and old people arrive to be baptized, a few to confess their sins, and young couples turn up for the sacrament of matrimony. People with a hundred and one problems and heartaches come for intercession before the icon of the most holy Mother of God.

Indeed, many people today prefer to visit a monastery or convent for the purpose of worshipping and obtaining a sacrament. The faithful prefer to go to church far from their daily environment of the megapolis, and far from their parish. Yet others, weighed down by the heavy cross of many unanswered questions, are drawn towards the monasteries in the hope of hearing a word of truth, a word of comfort, a word of love. Without, of course, forgetting that in many of the new city districts there are no parish churches.

That particular Sunday, I was not so much impressed by the crowd which had gathered or by the prayerfulness with which everybody accompanied the celebration of the divine liturgy. Engraved in my memory is the scene of four godparents with babies in their arms, and of a young couple, who hastily gathered round the baptismal font immediately after the liturgy. The young couple was founding a family. And since both the young man and the young woman most likely came from unbelieving families and had consequently not been baptized in time, they came first to be baptized and then to receive the church's blessing on their future family life.

Before those sacraments were celebrated, two more children, a young man and, finally, yet another child joined the group round the font. Altogether ten christenings were celebrated that blessed day at the convent of the Dormition. And there must be many other convents and monasteries where, every Sunday, a similar number of christenings, weddings and other sacraments are celebrated...

Our monasteries have thus been turned into oases of spiritual life. The monks and nuns are today engaged in most important missionary work within our community — the work of Christian witness and spiritual diakonia, the work of evangelizing. However, in spite of all their efforts and good will, they are not numerous enough and do not have sufficient means at their disposal. In many instances, the spiritual hunger of the people cannot be assuaged. The questions brought about by the way of life and the structures of our society, the existential quests and the interest shown in the word of God are increasing. That is why, in citing the missionary work of the religious and the monasteries, we dare use the word "oasis", knowing perfectly well the parts of the world where oases are found, and what needs they can cover...

What is the real cause of this interest in the monasteries and convents? Why do the faithful flock to them all without exception but with a preference for the big ones, which have greater means at their disposal, or those where the grace of the holy Mother of God is particularly in evidence? Why has the interest in monasteries among both believers and unbelievers grown?

The explanation is perhaps much simpler than we might imagine. Within our secularized society, one can sense a weary disenchantment, the consequence of a purely worldly life-style, a consumer mentality, a secularized culture and spirituality. In this environment, monks and nuns give a different testimony and a concrete example to follow. Their witness is a living witness. They teach the gospel word with their own lives and an ascetic world-view; indeed, with the lives and the ascetic spirit of generations of monks and nuns.

The word of God refreshes human nature, and its vision of God's kingdom is consoling. Thus, an Orthodox monastery or convent, as a place where efforts are being made night and day to turn the word into life and the kingdom into an accessible reality, attracts interest.

If we then add the existence of holy shrines and icons, as well as the miracles that are accomplished with the help of divine grace, we can understand the great spiritual prestige the monasteries enjoy, and better assess their importance as missionary centres.

Our questions cannot, however, be limited only to matters concerning the monasteries and convents and their missionary task as such. There is no doubt that, in the history and tradition of the Orthodox church, mission is closely linked to asceticism, and that, even today, in all Orthodox countries the monasteries uphold the proclamation of the gospel message. Nevertheless, the church as the body of Christ is a very broad community, in which every eucharistic gathering and every faithful believer is called upon to take part in the transmission of the joyful tidings.

For this reason, we must continue our questioning. To take just one example: what is the meaning of this flock going to the monasteries instead of the parish churches, which are thus deprived of the presence of their members, and in which the remaining few believers do not have the joy of rubbing shoulders with each other during the celebration of the sacraments? For our church and people, what is the significance of this "rivalry" between the parish clergy and the monks? How far can we exploit its beneficial results? What are the true dimensions of the spiritual needs, which the monasteries alone cannot cover, but which require the missionary mobilization of the official church authorities?

I believe that the blessed moment, the "fullness of time", has come for us to ask one another these questions. The urgent issue today is to make ourselves aware of our duty and try conscientiously to carry it out.

"God's Servant"

SAW LU

In May 1973 I left Begon, my native village in Latputta Township, to attend the Pwo Karen Seminary in Rangoon. I worked hard at the seminary because of my great desire to study the Bible.

During the summer vacation of my second year, I had an opportunity to serve the Lord at Ohnshitgon village in Taikkyi township. The people in Ohnshitgon requested the Karens at Taikkyi to help them learn the Karen language.

Thra Saw Ah Bi, the evangelist in charge then in Taikkyi village, and Thra Saw Plo Eh, the pastor in Watali Nyauggon village, approached the pastor of the Pwo Karen Baptist church, the Rev. Mahn Thori, to help the villagers of Ohnshitgon. Mahn Thori asked me, and I readily agreed as I was a country-bred man willing to help my fellow villagers prosper. Thus, in March 1975, I found myself happily serving the Lord in Ohnshitgon.

Ohnshitgon is a cluster of 47 homes located three miles from the Rangoon-Prome road. In summer, people use bicycles and carts and poor people travel on foot. In the rainy season, they go in sampans and motor boats, and the poor wade through the water and the marshes. The river overflows its banks every year, for about 15 to 30 days. During the flood, those who own boats and fishing nets earn their living by fishing. The majority of the village's three-hundred people are poor, living from day to day on whatever they can make as daily wage earners. Most are illiterate; only a few own land.

The whole village is made up entirely of Pwo Karens; so I had to teach the villagers, mostly children and teenagers, using Pwo Karen books. As the children had to attend school in another village, it was rather troublesome for them. Since I saw the need for the construction of a primary school in the village itself, I urged the elders to build one.

It was a pleasure to be in the third-year class at the seminary. However, I was looking forward to the holidays when I would be able to carry out practical work again.

During my third year of study, however, I was selected as a representative from the Rangoon Baptist Pwo Karen Association to attend the refresher course in religious education in Maubin town. I regarded it as God's plan because I had the opportunity to hear the lectures of Saya Allen Saw U, secretary for urban rural mission of the Myanmar Council of Churches. His ideas were in line with what I had been doing at Ohnshitgon village, and it was most encouraging for me. That night I had a long conversation with him about rural progress.

In December 1975 I went with Saya Allen Saw U and held a Christmas concert in Ohnshitgon. We discussed the needs of the village and possibilities of further work in rural development, and we prayed for God's guidance.

When the summer vacation began, I eagerly hurried to Ohnshitgon village. I was very glad to see that the primary school had been built. I had the opportunity to teach religion both in Pwo Karen and Sgaw Karen not only to the Ohnshitgon children, but also to those from the neighbouring villages of Retho, Outsu, Watali and Nyauggon. Moreover, I tried to find ways to guide them in agriculture, poultry farming and health care.

Early in 1977 some churches invited me to become a pastor. However, I declined as I had no intention of becoming a pastor at this stage of my seminary career. I had decided to serve the Lord in the undeveloped rural areas. I didn't know that this service might disappoint my mother.

While I was sitting for my final examination in March 1977, I got a telegram from my mother telling me that my father had passed away. She sent for me, but I could not go back as I had to sit for the examination. The news made me downhearted, and it was difficult to think about work in the rural areas.

However, I placed everything in the hands of God. Instead of going home when the examination was over, I went to Ohnshitgon. I could not comfort my sad mother. I loved Ohnshitgon, and I had come to Ohnshitgon to discuss important matters. Only after that, I went home for a while to comfort my mother.

I understood very well that to be successful in the rural areas it was no use sitting in the office in the city and managing from there the affairs of people in the countryside. I was fully determined to be a real villager in Ohnshitgon.

The villagers gave me a warm welcome. However, some people who didn't like my work tried to create trouble; but as I dealt with them humbly and sweetly, they became very friendly.

Though I had dreamed of working happily and successfully in the rural areas, there were times when the goals I wanted to attain seemed to be far away, and it was a rather bitter experience. I thanked the association that supported me, but sometimes I was close to starvation, and I had to live in a cowshed.

Alone I shed tears and prayed. I remembered what some people asked me: "With what intention do you come to this village? How many do you expect to become Christian?" "My duty", I replied, "is to make the villagers more understanding about Christianity and to develop themselves."

Every time I felt overwhelmed by the poverty and deprivation all around me, I turned to the Lord in prayer to help me carry out the work patiently. Thus, I worked, although I did not know clearly what system I should follow.

Thra Saw Allen Saw U invited me to attend the URM training course held at Holy Cross in Rangoon in May 1977. To meet others working in the same field, committed to the same mission, I went down to Rangoon. The course was most helpful. Through it I understood more about the mission I had become involved in. I decided to serve in this mission all my life.

When I got back to Ohnshitgon, I was able to use the techniques I learned at the training course. Though successful to a certain extent, I was alone and sometimes felt dispirited. I prayed for more co-workers to join me.

After a few months Thra Allen Saw U arrived, and I was encouraged. He brought with him M. Ja Naw who visited me often and became a friend with whom I could work closely.

At that time there was no well in the village. The villagers depended on water from the stream and epidemics were not uncommon. In the summer of 1978 the villagers agreed to build a tank in the village. I invited volunteers from Pegu, Rangoon and also near-by places. They promptly responded to the call, and the tank was constructed on a plot of land measuring about one and a half acres donated by Daw Yay Geh of the village.

The volunteers from Pegu brought a considerable number of old books and magazines, which stirred up an interest in reading. Thus a small reading and study group came into existence. It was called Mya Kan Tha Sah Kyit Waing, meaning Study Group of the Emerald Tank.

Through fervent prayers, we got the money from the Urban Rural Mission to buy a much-needed pump for farming. Also a dam was built across a tributary of the Pegu Yoma. It provided a steady supply of water for their fields and their cattle. We also developed a small pisciculture project.

Formerly only rich people could enjoy such amenities, but by 1977 everyone in the village could benefit from them. As a result, the people's daily income increased, and the earnings from the fish-rearing were used to improve our literacy programme in Ohnshitgon.

Ohnshitgon village suffered from floods. The villagers had to depend mostly on the winter rice cultivation. With the use of water from the dam and the water pump, co-operative groups now sprung up to cultivate jute. Life was now easier for the people. A committee was formed to settle problems that might arise among the jute cultivators as well as other kinds of problems in the village.

At first there were no Christians in the village, but gradually I formed a Sunday school class and began worship services that were held in people's homes. Thus, everyone came to know and feel the love of God. The teenagers began to look up to God in prayer before they started anything, such as sitting for their examinations or ploughing the fields.

On Christmas day 1977, there were many happy social gatherings as well as open air preaching. The teenagers were so fervent that some even witnessed before the people about God's love and blessing. Thereby, many became spiritually strengthened, and it led to the baptism of three men. Today many villagers have come to understand the Christian faith and behaviour though they have not yet received baptism. Through prayer, an old woman who was bitten by a poisonous insect was cured. In the same way, a man with a broken arm was healed.

Another story of faith involved a man coming home from a funeral. After helping cremate the dead body, he was plagued by unseen supernatural beings, as they believed, so much so that he suffered greatly. It was unbearable for him. Physicians gave up as they could not question the restless victim.

I asked his family if they wanted me to help him. They agreed to let me cure him. I asked the victim: "Who do you think I am?" "God's servant," he replied. There were more than a hundred people watching. I placed the Bible on his head and prayed. He became calm and slept. We asked his family to allow me and my young companions to come and worship in their house. They gave us permission, and we went and worshipped there. Later we asked the victim about his suffering, and he said that he did not remember anything about it.

My family and I have served in Ohnshitgon for ten years in the fields of education, health, spiritual ministry and social uplift. Keeping Ohnshitgon village as the centre of our mission, we were able to extend our work to the neighbouring towns and villages in the Irrawaddy Division.

Thus I was able to give good reports to the various churches concerned with this mission. I shared my experience with others at the various convention meetings. I also gave lectures at Rangoon Pwo Karen seminary about what education could do in rural areas.

Labouring Side by Side in the Gospel (cf. Phil. 4:3)

GEORGES LEMOPOULOS

Recently I had the privilege of being part of an ecumenical team visiting Albania on behalf of the World Council of Churches and the Conference of European Churches. The country had gone through a long period of isolation and suffering and it was the first time that representatives of the ecumenical community were able to meet brothers and sisters in this first atheistic state of the world. After many years with no possibility of encounter and exchange, a small group of Christians were now able to meet their brothers and sisters, to hear their stories, to pray with them and share their concerns, hopes and expectations in their radically changing society. It was an unforgettable experience.

My troubles started when I got back to Geneva... Very understandably, I was asked about my impressions. I had to give a detailed report of what I had seen in Albania. Suddenly, I felt like a *medieval cartographer*! I realized that the borders and coasts, the mountains and plains, the lakes and rivers I would draw on my map might in no time look like a caricature. Indeed, in such a rapidly changing context, any socio-political analysis and any evaluation of the religious experience of people could become outdated in a few weeks. It is not easy to deal with life amidst realities such as ideological intransigence, political rigidity, unprecedented social and economic crisis, cultural and religious pluralism, etc. Many parameters are necessary to understand the past, many forces are influencing and shaping the present, and a number of unpredictable factors could influence the future.

In spite of all these, I was deeply aware that there could be something undeniably *authentic* in my report. Something that neither time nor any further changes could diminish or alter. On a map the representation of the seas and oceans, the continents and borders may differ according to the perspective of the person who makes it. But it is impossible to change the basic content of the map: the names of towns and villages, regions and countries. Thus, in my case too, what was authentic and what I could report with all certainty were the names of persons I met and their stories, the stories of those Christians whose life had been a silent, and yet uninterrupted, witness to the gospel of hope and joy. Neither time nor political, economic or social changes could diminish the value and authenticity of such personal testimonies.

But what has this Albanian experience to do with the present collection of stories on evangelism?

My answer is direct and simple. After so many years of common ecumenical commitment, this is the first attempt to bring together evangelism experiences from the Protestant, Roman Catholic and Orthodox backgrounds. The publication of these stories is all the more significant because, after years of theological discussions, and in spite of the growing awareness of the churches that "evangelization is the test of our ecumenical vocation", we still have tremendous difficulties to agree on a common definition or a common strategy for evangelism. Therefore, my effort to say something about the vision, the context, the method, and the aim of evangelism, as reflected throughout these stories, might well appear like the task of the medieval cartographer.

Yet, as in my Albanian experience, there is in this collection something unequivocally *authentic:* the personal testimonies, the names and the stories of those persons who went through deep existential and spiritual experiences, persons who met with the transforming power of the word of God and dedicated their life to the proclamation of the good news of salvation. Nobody can deny the value and authenticity of this.

Let me first try to highlight some meaningful elements in this authenticity. Then, I shall try to focus on why we have difficulties, as an ecumenical community, to talk about evangelism. In both cases, the stories and experiences presented in this collection will remain the main source of inspiration for my reflections.

Giving an account of the hope that is within us (cf. 1 Pet. 3:15)

Not all the stories give concrete responses or clear answers; not all are success stories with a happy ending. We are constantly reminded that it is not possible for us to assess the results of our efforts. The first word and the final word belong always to the Spirit of God, for only the Holy Spirit can radically change human lives and transform human impasse into a way leading to life. In addition, the stories do not intend to probe the mystery of salvation to its depths, to analyze or define the very nature of God. Their only conviction — at least as I have personally identified it — is that access to the mystery can be gained through experience, the experience one can have of the working of the Holy Spirit as revealed to us in the scriptures.

Finally, the stories underline the importance of personal commitment to the gospel of Jesus Christ and the fundamental role of local communities. They remind us constantly that there are many ways to share the good news of salvation, many ways to evangelize. There is almost a complete absence here of terms like "agencies", "strategies", "campaigns", "denominational aggrandizement", etc. The accent is rather on sharing, on "giving an account of the hope that is within us". Brothers and sisters share with simplicity and sincerity, what they have seen, heard and experienced (cf. Acts 4:20) in their meeting with the word of God or in their life within a worshipping and witnessing community. They are aware that the joy of such an experience becomes complete only when it is shared with others, so that they also might become communicants and participants (cf. 1 John 1:4).

The word of God lives and abides for ever (Pet. 1:23)

When reading these stories, one is really tempted to affirm that they mirror, above all, *the perennial freshness of the word* of God, its *unique value* in all ages and historical contexts. In other words, they mediate the gospel message and emphasize God's continuous presence in history and the lives of men and women.

The gospel invites us to a way of life, a mind-set, a spiritual perspective transcending time and space, historical and geographical frontiers, all racial and gender differences. It involves love for God and fellow human beings and a sacramental way of living. It calls us to faithful and self-sacrificing commitment. It leads to a creative tension between what we now are and what we can be tomorrow. But all these remain just words — empty words — if they are not experienced, if they do not become tangible realities today, in our lives and our witness. That experience is the strength of the stories included here.

The writers are not attempting to fill minds with facts; they are rather attempting to move hearts and minds with personal testimonies. The inherent risk of reducing the proclamation of the gospel to the imparting of information about the faith is effectively overcome. We discover people and communities who are characterized by zeal and enthusiasm for their faith, their community and their church. Here are no sermons meant to throw light on the meaning of a parable, a moment in the life of our Lord Jesus Christ or a certain aspect of the life of the early Christian community. Brothers and sisters living today in different parts of our world and facing different realities become the very protagonists of the parables and other biblical stories; they become both the subjects and objects of the existential meeting with the transforming power of the word of God; they try to share a vision of the kingdom which gives meaning and direction to the whole of life.

To illustrate this, let us take some examples. There are many ways for preaching on the well known — and sometimes over-used — parable of the sower (Matt. 13:3ff.; Mark 4:1ff.; Luke 8:4ff. and 5:1ff.). And yet, it is really amazing to read how a Polish young man discovered in this parable — and here allow me the use of secular expressions — the *guiding principle* and the *basic scenario* for his life and witness. Such a personal experience certainly adds another dimension to our reading of the gospel as well as to our commitment to it. Similarly, there are many ways of studying the life of the early Christian community in the Book of the Acts: the conversions and baptisms, the sharing of bread and of other resources, the founding of Christian homes, the joy of worship and the spread of the gospel that resulted from persecutions. Reading here about the daily life and witness of an Orthodox monastery in Bulgaria, we are brought back to almost identical experiences taking place here and now, close to us both in terms of time and of space.

Sonny Teresa's story, perhaps, is the most significant example. In hermeneutics, as well as in our spirituality, we often have difficulties to discern what Christ's temptation in the desert could mean for us today. Maybe, without realizing it, Sonny Teresa provides an excellent theological response.

"Command this stone to become bread," said the tempter to Jesus. And Sonny Teresa reports to us her struggle with her own temptation and her effort to escape suffering and enjoy comfort. She wants to justify — in fact to transform into *bread of life* — her daily experiences: her eating and drinking, her smoking and dancing, her social and sexual behaviour. Very simply, after a long journey, she discovers that human beings "shall not live by bread alone"!

"Then the devil took Jesus up and showed him all the kingdoms of the world in a moment of time, and said to him: 'To you I will give all this authority and their glory.'" Coming from Iran to Europe, Sonny Teresa discerns the possibility of sharing in such authority and glory through a cultural, social or political conversion. She looks for security without faith. She is tempted to adopt the values of the kingdom in which she lives now. Many are those who encourage her to do so, while others strongly criticize her and treat her as a hypocrite. She struggles until she discovers that "you shall worship the Lord your God, and him only shall you serve"!

"Throw yourself down from here," said the tempter to Jesus, "for it is written: 'He will give his angels charge of you, to guard you', and 'on their hand they will bear you up, lest you strike your foot against a stone.'" This is our eternal temptation: to prove our supernatural powers, our capacity for working miracles, and of exercising dominion over the whole creation. Here too Sonny Teresa is no exception. She dreams of a golden fish jumping out of the pool and flying at her command. She asks for a proof and immediately she receives it. Nevertheless, in spite of this proof, her questions remain unanswered and her anguish unassuaged. She has to struggle again and again with herself until she becomes convinced that "you shall not tempt the Lord your God"!

One gets the impression that Sonny Teresa — like many others in the stories — being evangelized becomes simply and naturally an evangelist; she radiates the ever-fresh quality of the gospel and the transforming power of the word of God.

...not to condemn the world, but to save the world... (John 12:47)

This *transforming power of the word of God* is the second important point that struck me in reading the stories. I felt that in many cases people were ready to leave the *terra firma* — or what they believed to be so — of their life-styles and convictions and to seek the source of all life. Of course, such a change — almost a self-renunciation — is not easy.

Let us take the example of that young Buddhist girl living in the USA. "Her mother was seriously ill", we read, "and one day, in desperation, she had prayed: 'Jesus, can you hear me? My mother is dying. I heard over the radio a preacher say that you are the living Lord Jesus who heals. So please heal my mother. I want her.'" It was impossible to read this short account without making a connection with the Roman centurion (Matt. 8:5). He also had vaguely heard about Jesus. He also had his own convictions, plus power and authority. He sensed, however, the possibility of a real transformation in his life and the life of his household.

A real transformation is possible not only on the level of personal lives, but also in the lives of communities, societies and cultures. It is true that Jesus told the Samaritan woman of "a spring of water welling up to eternal life" (John 4:14). But one cannot forget the fact that long ago, Jacob had provided a well for his people.

We need not deal with the many dimensions of meaning in this passage. I am deeply convinced, however, that most of them are present in Saw Lu's story. In the small Muslim village of Ohnshitgon in Burma, Saw Lu started his evangelistic witness following the example of Jacob rather than of Jesus. As there was no well in the village, he convinced people to build a tank. Then, through the Urban Rural Mission, they got a pump to help with their farming. There was no water for the fields and the cattle. The poor villagers earned more money. A pisciculture project was set up and the money earned through it was used to improve education. Life became easier for the whole village. Indeed, life was transformed....

Another example. What is reported in several stories about the healing power of the word is certainly of extreme importance. But the healing — and even the non-healing in some cases — as such never constitutes the heart of the message. The most important point here is how we share in the pain and suffering of our fellow human beings and — even more important — how we respond to a person with a serious health problem or a conspicuous handicap. Are we ready to admit that sickness is related to sin? Are we ready to confess that, according to Christ, sickness is bondage to the devil? If so, we may extend our understanding to other suffering brothers and sisters: the weak, the poor, the oppressed, the victims of injustice. Then, the real transformation is not only that of the persons who suffer, but our own as well, as we learn that with Jesus Christ the forgiveness of sins, the healing of the body, the driving out of the devil — here "the prince of this world" (John 12:31) is the devil — and the raising of the dead are all one and the same act of existential transformation, ultimately of salvation.

God's love has been poured into our hearts... (Rom. 5:5)

If we can speak about this existential quest, it is because *God's love is ever manifested in the world* and experienced in many different situations. And this is the third important aspect of the stories. Not only do they affirm that God by nature "is love" (1 John 4:8), but also underline that nothing one can do will make God stop loving us.

A Coptic Orthodox family in Egypt experiences God's love in its daily life, as the members are called to participate in the liturgical and sacramental life of their church and to be ever renewed through the forgiving and healing power of the Holy Spirit. For two young men in Russia, pondering over their place in this world, this love is of the utmost importance, especially in the midst of "a wild materialistic pseudo-culture". "It was becoming clear to us", one of them says, "that the Lord was alive, that we loved him and had not forgotten him, even as he had loved us and had not forgotten us."

Far from Russia, in one of the widely scattered Maasai villages, Ng'oto Rachel, a widow, with no son to care for her and therefore lacking any status, discovers in the gospel that through Christ she is a daughter, a child of God. "She knows that Jesus loves her and gave his life to bring her to God." Jesus teaches us that God's supreme joy is to have us live near him, as sons and daughters. God loves every human being without condition. He loves all of us and each of us as we are, and seeks to guide us by his love into his kingdom.

Your hearts will rejoice, and no one will take the joy from you (John 16:22)

Last but not least, the stories reflect *an extraordinary joy*. A joy experienced in all circumstances, even amidst difficulties, tears and sorrows. Needless to say this joy has nothing to do with ordinary happiness, pleasure or fun. It is rather the "joy in believing" (Rom. 15:13). It is the joy of knowing the freedom of truth in the love of God (cf. John 8:32). It is also the joy of being made worthy to "share in Christ's sufferings" (1 Pet. 4:13).

Reading the stories one after the other, I was thinking of what the late Fr Alexander Schmemann had written about the joy of a Christian: "Christianity has been the proclamation of joy, of the only possible joy on earth. It rendered impossible all joy we usually think of as possible. But within this impossibility, at the very bottom of this darkness, it announced and conveyed a new all-embracing joy, and with this joy it transformed the End into a Beginning. Without the proclamation of this joy, Christianity is incomprehensible. It is only as joy that the church was victorious in the world, and it lost the world when it lost that joy, and ceased to be a credible witness to it. Of all accusations against Christians, the most terrible one was uttered by Nietzsche when he said that Christians had no joy."

No! This is not true! Christians do have joy! It is the joy of an old and extremely poor Chinese lady who dies in Malaysia in all dignity, in the arms of Jesus the Lord she had heard about so many years ago. It is the joy of a Roman Catholic priest in Bangladesh working in the rice fields as a member of Mazam Ali's family, receiving one meal a day and sometimes two. It is the joy of Edith, an evangelist in Ghana, when she sees the spiritual growth of the communities she had started, sometimes with only one person or two who were illiterate or had few years of formal education. It is the joy of a young Armenian priest discovering through the gospel the roots of his family, nation and culture, his roots which are established in God! It is the joy of young Orthodox in Poland praying, singing, discussing and experiencing the joy of Easter as they greet one another with the traditional Easter greeting: "Christ is risen!" "Indeed, he is risen!"

And now, let me conclude this part of my reflections on our stories with another story... God sent out two angels, each bearing a large basket, to gather people's prayers. The angels came to earth and one began to collect petitions, the other thanksgivings. One of the baskets, the one containing petitions — requests, appeals and complaints — was soon full and overflowing. The other, the one containing thanksgivings, was practically empty...

Personally, I am deeply grateful to the authors of the stories presented here for they wanted to contribute to the second basket! The whole book seems to be an endless thanksgiving. People's experiences are offered to God with the realization that they are God's gifts to them. In my Orthodox theological language I would say that throughout the book one can discern the eucharistic prayer, when the celebrant — echoing David's prayer (cf. 2 Chron. 29:19) — says: "We offer you, Lord, these gifts from your own gifts, for all things and in all circumstances"!

Evangelism is not a solitary way...

I come now to the most difficult part of my task. The enthusiasm created by the first reading gives way to a critical approach. I would be really happy if by any chance I could stop my reading at the very personal level of our stories, at the authenticity of personal testimonies. I know, however, that this is impossible.

In every single page of the gospel, a personal story, a crucial moment in the life of some man and woman, even the deepest experience of a personal conversion, all are clearly related to the life of the community, are not cut off from the concrete historical and cultural context, are always understood within the framework of the surrounding socio-political realities.

In other words, names of cities and villages are extremely important for a map; but they are not sufficient by themselves. It is absolutely necessary to include also the borders and coasts. Similarly, the most fundamental Christian act of proclaiming the good news of salvation cannot be understood without its theological, ecclesiological, cultural, socio-political and relational implications.

It is true that churches today agree without any hesitation that "at the very heart of the church's vocation in the world is the proclamation of the kingdom of God inaugurated in Jesus the Lord, crucified and risen". Undoubtedly, this unites all churches. Nevertheless, the ways and methods of evangelism, the aim and purpose of the evangelistic witness, the theological and sacramental foundation of the proclamation still create tensions among churches, confessional families and theological traditions.

I am afraid our stories do not provide answers to many questions. They simply highlight the basic difficulties of the present ecumenical effort and focus on some crucial issues underlining our obstacles and deadlocks. I will try to respect this spirit, remain faithful to this option and will not make any effort to "theologize" on this particular aspect of the stories. I would like, therefore, to conclude by simply reporting here some challenges addressed to our ecumenical reflection and our involvement in offering a common witness to the world.

One of the stories (from Egypt) affirms that "the proclamation of the gospel in the church is a sacramental act, a form of communion with God, a real mystery in and through which people feel united with God". Have we sufficiently explored the sacramental dimension of evangelism, the relation between the sacraments of the word and the table? Have we underlined that both in the gospel and in the sacrament Jesus Christ is continually offering himself as "the way, the truth and the life" (John 14:6)?

Another story (from Malaysia) draws our attention to the fact that "more often than not it seems to be the warmth of the Christian community and Christians at worship together which attracts people and ultimately convinces them to put their faith in Christ". Is it possible to dissociate our biblical vision from its manifestation in the liturgical life of the community? Have we sufficiently appreciated the fact that proclamation should not be taken only in the narrow sense of an informative preaching of the truth, but also in the sense of incorporating humanity into the mystical union with God? What is the relation between the evangelistic witness and the ecclesial reality?

As far as our relations to other religious traditions and other cultures are concerned, one of the stories (from Great Britain) reminds us that "evangelism is through a 'kenotic' ministry, emptied of self but listening, ready to answer but not speaking first, loving for the sake of him who loved us and praying as if life itself depended on it: like John the Baptist, pointing always to Jesus who is the key to the understanding of God, the universe and humanity". In all humility we need to confess that, as the ecumenical family, we have a long and difficult way ahead of us in order to grow together in our understanding of other faiths and cultures.

"Labouring side by side in the gospel" (cf. Phil. 4:3) — that title was inspired by what is said in one of the stories (from Kenya), where the need — and the challenge — for a common commitment in proclaiming the gospel today is clearly underlined. Let me conclude with these words: "Evangelism is not a solitary way; it is walking the narrow path with fellow Christians, enduring with them the thorns, the rocks, the heat — even the mud and the manure of life — yet joining with them in the joy of service, sharing with them the tasks of everyday life, singing with them a song of praise for the water of life, freely offered by our Lord Jesus Christ".

Contributors

James K. Agbeblewu is chairman of the executive committee of the Volta Evangelistic Association, Ghana.

Dr Maurice Assad is associate general secretary of the Middle East Council of Churches.

Dr Ivan Tselev Dimitrov is professor of biblical theology at the Theological Faculty of Sofia, Bulgaria.

Deacon Hagop Dingilian is a minister in the Armenian Apostolic Church, Etchmiadzin.

Dr Marion Fairman, from the USA, is a nurse, missionary and writer of religious plays.

Robert Hunt was with the Malaysian Theological Seminary in Kuala Lumpur.

Graham Kings, formerly with the Anglican parish of Harlesden, London, is now on the staff of St Andrew's Institute for Mission and Evangelism, Kabare, in the diocese of Mount Kenya East.

Dr Slawomir Makal, from Poland, is an engineer specialized in the field of space research.

Father Robert McCahill is a Maryknoll father who served for a period in Bangladesh.

Rev. Theodore H. Perera is founder and minister-in-charge of Dev Suwa Sevawa in Moratuwa, Sri Lanka.

Saw Lu (no information available).

Shirley Shultz served as assistant pastor of the United Christian Church in Levittown, PA, USA, until September 1992, when she entered a clinical pastoral education programme at a local hospital.

Archpriest Ioann Sviridov is a priest of the Russian Orthodox Church in Moscow.

Father Douglas Venne is a Maryknoll father who served for a period in Bangladesh.

Rev. Dr John Watson is the director of the Centre for the Study of Christianity in Islamic Lands, England.